MIND AND BRAIN

A Dialogue on the Mind-Body Problem

Second Edition

MIND AND BRAIN

A Dialogue on the Mind-Body Problem

Second Edition

Rocco J. Gennaro

Hackett Publishing Company, Inc.
Indianapolis/Cambridge

For further information, please address
     Hackett Publishing Company, Inc.
     P.O. Box 44937
     Indianapolis, Indiana 46244-0937

     www.hackettpublishing.com

Cover design by Deborah Wilkes
Cover art by Jolygon, Shutterstock #1033250638
Composition by Aptara, Inc.

Library of Congress Control Number: 2019952372

ISBN-13: 978-1-62466-854-8 (pbk.)

CONTENTS

INTRODUCTION

This is a substantially revised and updated edition of my dialogue of the same title first published in 1996. It is an introduction to the mind-body problem and is intended for use in undergraduate courses in philosophy, psychology, and cognitive science. It can also be used in graduate courses as a supplementary reading. Its purpose is to develop some of the views and arguments that have emerged in the literature. For those not familiar with the philosophy of mind, the dialogue aims to provide an overview of the key issues; it can also serve as a summary for those with a broader background. No prior knowledge of philosophy is required.

There are three characters and "three nights" of debate or conversation. The reader can easily remember which position each participant holds by the first letter of their names; Mary is the materialist, Dave is a substance dualist, Steve is rather skeptical of both views. The First Night covers (1) the overall "mind-body problem" and its connection to the issue of immortality; (2) some scientific advantages of materialism; (3) a critical discussion of Descartes' "Divisibility Argument" for substance dualism; and (4) a critical discussion of what is called the "Argument from Introspection" for substance dualism.

The Second Night covers (1) problems with dualism concerning the interaction between the mind and the brain; (2) the relation between brain damage and the prospect of an afterlife; (3) a critical discussion of parallelism and epiphenomenalism; (4) the so-called type-token distinction within materialism and the problem of multiple realizability; and (5) a discussion of Thomas Nagel's and Frank Jackson's arguments aimed at showing that materialism cannot fully explain consciousness. Property dualism and panpsychism are also briefly discussed.

The Third Night focuses on the more epistemological "problem of other minds." I examine (1) the difference between inductive and certain knowledge; (2) how the problem changes depending on whether the "other mind" is human, animal, alien, or machine; (3) various kinds of evidence which might help to determine whether another creature has a conscious mind, such as behavior and brain structure; and (4) a version of the so-called inverted spectrum argument.

Key terms or principles are printed in **bold** and are defined in the glossary. Other emphasized words are in *italics*. There are also numerous study questions and a selected bibliography with suggested further readings at the end of this book.

I would like to thank Deborah Wilkes of Hackett Publishing Company for her support of this project.

MIND AND BRAIN

A Dialogue on the Mind-Body Problem

This is a record of conversations among three first-year philosophy graduate students about the nature of the mind. The conversations take place in a graduate student pub over three nights. Mary, a materialist, is arguing with Dave, a dualist, about the relevance of their beliefs to the issue of immortality. Steve, who is generally skeptical of both positions and less certain of his own view, joins Mary and Dave later.

THE FIRST NIGHT

1.1 The Mind-Body Problem: Materialism vs. Dualism

Mary and Dave are sitting at a table in the pub. Dave notices that Mary seems a little distracted.

DAVE: What's up, Mary? Anything wrong?

MARY: Well, yeah, I found out just yesterday that my cousin Tom died after a short battle with cancer. He was only thirty years old. It's difficult for everyone in the family to accept. They are planning a funeral for some time next week back home in New York.

DAVE: I'm very sorry. I know how you feel to some extent. My aunt died of leukemia last year. We all miss her terribly, but she's always with me in some ways. Perhaps you can take some comfort in the idea that Tom is at peace or perhaps in Heaven. I know you aren't religious, but maybe you still believe in an afterlife or God in some sense?

MARY: No. There are many reasons why I don't believe in God. For one, I have a difficult time understanding why a supposedly all-knowing, all-powerful, and all-good Being would allow so much misery and evil to exist in the world. I know that theists have responses to this "problem of evil," but they haven't convinced me with those free will and greater good replies. But, anyway, that's not really the main reason for my atheism.

DAVE: What *is* your main reason, then?

Mary: Since I don't believe in immortality, I find it difficult to believe in God, especially as represented in the Western conception of God. I mean, if our death really is the end, then why believe in God? What would be the point? I think that a belief in immortality is prior to a belief in God. *Psychologically* speaking, I think that it's mainly the desire for continued life after bodily death that ultimately leads most people to believe in God.

Dave: Maybe; that's hard to say.

Mary: I do know, of course, that there are independent philosophical *arguments* for God's existence, but that's a different issue. I think they fail to establish the existence of God for other reasons. But what I am saying is that, as a matter of psychological fact, a belief in immortality is often the main motivation for a belief in God. I can understand and try to respect it, but I don't think it stands up to reason. It would of course be nice if there were some sort of blissful existence in an afterlife, but I think the evidence is to the contrary and wishful thinking isn't a rational basis for such a belief.

Dave: I think there are good independent reasons to believe in God, but I'm curious about your reasoning here. Since your atheism derives mainly from your rejection of immortality, why do you think there is no afterlife?

Mary: Mainly because I am a **materialist** about the human mind; that is, I believe that all mental processes are simply brain processes or states. In short, the mind is the brain.

Dave: How exactly do you then conclude that there is no immortality?

Mary: Well, what is it that continues on after bodily death? Clearly, it is supposed to be one's thoughts, memories, beliefs, experiences, and so on. And isn't this just what we mean by the term 'mind'? But if the mind is basically the brain, then at death it must cease to exist and function. To put it bluntly: it eventually rots away with the rest of the body so there cannot be immortality. I'd say the same is true for all animals on the planet.

Dave: I follow your reasoning, but aren't you confusing the mind with the soul? I believe it's the soul that survives bodily death.

MARY: When we describe what is supposed to be immortal, it still sounds like what we mean by the mind. I defy you to explain any coherent distinction between the mind and the soul. As a matter of fact, these terms are used interchangeably in many historical texts, and, for example, both English words have been used to translate the single Greek word *psyche.* Granted, sometimes the term 'soul' carries a more theological connotation in that the Greek word *nous* could also be translated as 'soul,' but it doesn't follow that the words 'soul' and 'mind' refer to entirely different things.

DAVE: I'll accept your equation of 'mind' with 'soul' for the sake of argument, but I'm not sure there's no difference. For example, I believe that infants, fetuses, and severely mentally challenged people have souls that are just as real and whole as yours or mine. But clearly their minds are not like yours and mine. I think that animals have minds, but not souls.

MARY: So there are three things associated with each human being: a mind, a soul, and a body?

DAVE: Yes. On second thought, you may be right that there are only two.

MARY: It sounds unnecessarily crowded in your view of human beings. I have a hard time accepting such a position, especially if you want to hold that the mind or the soul or both are nonphysical in some way. Is this what you think?

DAVE: Yes. I am a **substance dualist**: I believe that the mind and the body are distinct substances, and that the mind is a nonphysical substance.

MARY: Do you again see how the mind sounds like the soul?

DAVE: Sure. I said I'd grant that to you for the sake of argument. But you see, of course, why I believe in immortality. If my mind is nonphysical, then it can continue to exist without my body and therefore can survive bodily death. I realize that it's more difficult for you to believe in immortality given your materialism. Perhaps we should focus on our fundamental disagreement about the nature of human minds. But first I want to be clear: Are you saying that if materialism is true, it is *impossible* to believe in life after death?

Mary: Not quite, but immortality becomes extremely unlikely. I suppose it's still possible, for example, that our bodies or just our brains are somehow brought back to life, or are duplicated and made to function as before. This would be a way for our minds to persist, but we certainly have no reason to believe that this happens upon bodily death.

Dave: OK, but if you believed in God you might think that He does that, and He transports all of the bodies or brains to some other physical place forever. This is not what I believe happens, but it's at least a possible way for a materialist to believe in immortality. It would be based on the idea of bodily resurrection, which obviously has biblical significance. I'm pretty sure this is what the philosopher Peter van Inwagen believes.

Mary: Perhaps it's remotely possible, but it still seems very unlikely. Anyway, it's not what either of us thinks happens to other animals, so why should I think it happens only when human beings die? Also, you are presupposing that God exists in order to perform such miracles and, as I mentioned, I'm an atheist mainly because I'm a materialist. So using God's existence in your reasoning here is not at all convincing to me.

Dave: Fine, but you see my point.

Mary: Of course; maybe it would be better to discuss in a more direct fashion why you're a dualist and why I'm a materialist since this seems to be the key issue.

Dave: Sure. Where would you like to start?

Mary: Well, I know of no really good arguments for substance dualism, but I think there are many good philosophical and scientific reasons favoring materialism.

Dave: I have a couple of philosophical arguments for **dualism**, but first let me hear your scientific reasons supporting materialism. This is most certainly a central problem in **metaphysics**.

1.2 Scientific Support for Materialism

MARY: *First*: Although some religious views call evolution into question, I certainly believe in the evolution of species. And only materialism makes sense in this context.

DAVE: You're right that I'm sometimes a bit skeptical of evolutionary theory. It seems more speculative compared to other scientific claims. At the very least, evolutionary theory still doesn't explain the origin of life itself. There are some disputes about various key details as well and we all know how often science has been mistaken in the past. Generally, however, theism and evolution are at least logically compatible. But, anyway, even if evolution occurred pretty much in the way you believe, why would materialism follow?

MARY: Do you believe that a cat has a mind?

DAVE: Sure.

MARY: How about dogs, tigers, and chimps?

DAVE: Of course, just not minds as advanced as ours.

MARY: Do you believe they survive bodily death? That there is a dog heaven or a chimp heaven? That their minds are distinct nonphysical substances?

DAVE: No to all three questions.

MARY: So then somehow magically we're the only creatures on earth who have a nonphysical substance associated with us? And just how did such an amazing thing happen in the evolutionary process? I mean if animal minds are just their brains, why are we so different? How and why did nonphysical minds slip into the picture between apes and us?

DAVE: I can't answer that in a purely scientific way partly because I don't accept that everything must be explained so scientifically.

MARY: OK, but this brings me to my *second* general reason in favor of materialism. If materialism is true, it's at least possible to explain mental functioning in terms of the brain. On the other hand, if dualism is true, then it would be impossible to observe or to scientifically examine the mind. You must admit that in this sense materialism has a general advantage.

DAVE: Not really. If materialism is true, it does have the advantage in the *scientific* investigation of the mind. But this alone is not a good enough reason to believe that materialism is true.

MARY: Perhaps not, but together with my earlier point about evolution, it seems rather powerful.

DAVE: I disagree; but do you have another general argument in support of materialism?

MARY: Sure, here is the *third*: You're familiar with the **principle of simplicity** often used in scientific debate. I have yet another argument based on brain damage cases, but maybe we can get back to that one later or tomorrow.

DAVE: OK, but, yes, I know the principle of simplicity. It says that if there are two theories both of which explain the same number of observations or facts, then we should accept the one that posits fewer objects or the one that is simpler. For example, in astronomy, once we had the alternative simpler theory of elliptical orbits, we came to realize that bizarre and complicated planetary motions weren't needed to explain our observations. And there are all kinds of other substances that no longer have any validity for similar reasons, such as ether.

MARY: Right, and the same goes here. Even assuming that dualism could explain as much about the mind as materialism, which is really impossible, why accept the theory that posits an extra mysterious nonphysical entity when the brain will do just as well? Shouldn't we accept materialism on grounds of simplicity alone?

DAVE: Perhaps, but only within the confines of a scientific debate. The principle of simplicity is, as you mentioned, a scientific principle, and I'm not sure that it should apply to metaphysical issues like the mind-body problem, especially since questions about the soul and immortality are at stake.

MARY: But at least materialists have a chance at scientifically understanding the mind whereas dualism leaves us with no hope at all.

DAVE: Maybe, but I find it incredible that the wet, slimy, gray and white stuff in your skull just *is* your mind. You make it sound so obvious, but do you really believe that neurochemical processes in your brain just *are* your thoughts, pains, fears, loves, and so on? You talk about the "magic" of a nonphysical soul. Well, that sounds like just as much magic to me.

MARY: It's not magic or mysterious; it's the very complicated workings of a very complex organ. Any good materialist will concede that we know comparatively little about how the brain produces conscious mentality, but at least we are learning, whereas dualism offers no hope whatsoever for scientific investigation. Give us time and we'll have a good scientific explanation of how mental states are constituted by neural states. Much is already known about which areas of the brain are responsible for which mental function, not to mention how much is known about how neurons work and interconnect. There have been many apparently mysterious or "magical" phenomena which are eventually explained scientifically.

DAVE: I think you're incredibly optimistic about the mind and consciousness. But, more importantly, you accuse me of having an unfounded faith in immortality and God, while you seem to express a kind of "faith" in scientific knowledge and progress.

MARY: I wouldn't call it 'faith' because it's based more on scientific evidence. Also, you agreed that animal minds are purely physical and can be identified with their brains. So if a cat's fear that it will be chased by the dog is a purely physical process in the cat's brain, then why do you find it so hard to believe that human mental states are also just brain processes? Granted, we don't currently have all the answers about how the brain accomplishes what it does, but it surely seems reasonable to think that it alone is responsible for mental functioning.

DAVE: Perhaps it all comes back to my theological belief in an immortal soul.

MARY: But you said you wouldn't rely on that for the sake of argument.

DAVE: Fair enough, but I'm convinced there's a deeper problem with materialism and just how well it can explain consciousness. As a matter of fact, this reminds me of Steve, who's just walked in. He's somewhat skeptical about materialism, although he's at least equally doubtful of dualism.

Hey, Steve, come on over here!

Steve joins Dave and Mary at their table.

STEVE: Hey, you two, sorry I'm late. What'd I miss?

DAVE: Not much. We've been arguing the case of materialism versus dualism.

STEVE: Well, I know you're the dualist, Dave. That means Mary must be the materialist.

MARY: Brilliant deduction, Steve.

STEVE: For various reasons, I'm skeptical of both positions. But I don't want to take over conversation. What were you discussing?

MARY: I've finished explaining what I take to be various scientific and theoretical advantages of materialism. We should also keep in mind that this is not merely some theoretical exercise; for example, an anesthesiologist needs to be able to determine scientifically whether or not a surgical patient is conscious from an outside scientific perspective. I mean, suppressing consciousness and especially pain, without killing the patient, is obviously the rather important job of an anesthesiologist. Maybe that's why their malpractice insurance is so high! There's clearly a very practical aspect to this matter. Much the same goes for end-of-life consciousness and related ethical issues, such as when a patient is in a coma or a persistent vegetative state.

DAVE: Sure, but what about **near-death experiences** (NDEs)? They're sometimes also mentioned as providing some evidence for dualism and immortality. Some patients, often in cardiac arrest at a hospital, experience a peaceful moving through a tunnellike structure to a light and are often able to see doctors working on their bodies while hovering over them in an emergency room, a sort of **out-of-body experience** (OBE). These are frequently very moving emotional experiences that have a profound effect on patients. In some cases, the patient even sees other deceased relatives and exhibits very little brain activity.

MARY: I don't doubt that they have the experiences, but what actually causes them and how to interpret them is the real question. Materialists will point out that NDEs can be artificially induced in various experimental situations and also that starving the brain of oxygen is known to cause hallucinations. This "dying brain hypothesis" is also bolstered by the knowledge that the release of endorphins, a brain chemical, during times of stress and fear can explain the feelings of peacefulness.

STEVE: And we do have to remember that NDEs are supposed to be "near death" experiences not "after death," and so some brain activity is presumably still present during the time of the NDE. Of course, if it could ever be shown that one is having a conscious experience *at a time* when there is *no* brain activity then there would be strong evidence for dualism. I'm not, however, aware that this has ever been documented or even how it could be conclusively shown. Also, some mystical and religious experiences share the features of NDEs and some others result from temporal lobe epilepsy.

MARY: Good point, Steve. And I was just reading the other day that out-of-body experiences can be induced by stimulating neurons in the right side of the temporal lobe area called the temporo parietal junction.

STEVE: Now that is very interesting.

MARY: Anyway, I think Dave was planning to offer a couple of philosophical arguments for dualism.

STEVE: I'm all ears.

MARY: Me too. Give it your best shot, Dave.

1.3 The Divisibility Argument and Leibniz's Law

DAVE: I can think of many arguments, but I'll restrict myself to two of the more interesting ones. The first is my favorite traditional argument from Descartes, but I need to set it up first.

MARY: Sure.

DAVE: If I could show you that there is a property that the brain has but the mind does not have, or vice versa, wouldn't you both have to accept the conclusion that the mind cannot be identical with the brain?

MARY: I suppose so. Wouldn't that follow from **Leibniz's Law**?

DAVE: Yes.

STEVE: Wait, what exactly is Leibniz's Law?

DAVE: It's a principle about identity which says that "if an object or event x is identical with an object or event y, then x and y have all of the same properties." So if x and y have any different properties, then x cannot be identical with y. The issue is whether we have two different objects or really just two different names which refer to one object.

STEVE: So the issue is whether or not the terms 'mind' and 'brain' refer to the same thing, or whether they name distinct objects. And if one object has a property that the other lacks, then they must be distinct. Therefore, dualism would be true and materialism false.

DAVE: Right. There are of course countless examples of two terms or expressions naming the same thing.

MARY: Yes, like the terms 'water' and 'H$_2$O' or the 'Morning Star' and 'Venus.' The two expressions need not *mean* the same thing, but they *refer* to only one object. This is the way I think of the terms 'mind' and 'brain,' or, for example, 'pain' and 'neural state x.' There is really only one object or event.

DAVE: But if one object has a property the other lacks, then they cannot be identical. My aim is to show that minds or mental states have properties, which brains do not have, or vice versa, and so they are not identical.

MARY: Well, what property do you think can demonstrate this?

DAVE: Divisibility. To paraphrase Descartes: My body is divisible, since it can be separated. For example, my arm or my finger can be cut off and my brain can be cut in half. In short, my body has parts. On the other hand, when I think to myself about my mind, I cannot understand the idea that my mind is divisible. I can't understand my mind 'split' in any way analogous to my body. Can I understand my current thought divided, say, in half? No. Does it have a left half and a right half? Of course not. So the mind must be distinct from the brain. The latter has a property, divisibility, which the former lacks.

Maybe we should put it formally so we can more easily keep it in mind. Let's call it the Divisibility Argument (*Dave writes the following argument down*):

(1) My body, which includes my brain, is divisible.
(2) I cannot conceive of my mind as divisible.
Therefore, (3) my mind is distinct from any part of my body.

STEVE: In premise 2, aren't you just assuming that the mind is non-physical? This would be begging the question: assuming what you are trying to prove; namely, that dualism is true. After all, if materialism is true, then my mind can be divided in the same way that any part of my body can be.

DAVE: No, I'm not begging the question. I'm just reporting something that seems obvious when I introspect; namely, that my mind is not divisible. I'm just saying that when I think about my own mind, I cannot conceive of it as a divisible thing.

MARY: OK, but there is something odd about the term 'divisible.' If you mean 'can be split up,' then you might be begging the question against the materialist. So I assume you mean something more like 'has parts'?

DAVE: Yes, and I believe that is closer to Descartes' original meaning. So, now what's the problem?

MARY: Well, even when I introspect my mind, I think I can understand it as having parts, and so premise 2 would be false. It has
parts such as my memories, my beliefs, my fears, my desires, and
so on. In short, I think of my mind as having compartments con-
taining different types of mental states. They are the parts that
compose my mind. If my mind is a bundle of mental states, then
the mental states are the parts. Why isn't that 'conceiving of my
mind as divisible'?

DAVE: But aren't you now begging the question? That is, assuming
materialism to be true?

MARY: I don't think so. What I said doesn't presuppose either position. If anything, you're assuming dualism by assuming that a nonphysical thing cannot have parts.

DAVE: Again, for the reason given earlier, I don't think so.

STEVE: But, Mary, I recall Descartes saying something in reply to
your claim that you can conceive of your mind as divisible; that
is, as having parts or compartments such as beliefs, desires, and
so on.

MARY: What was it?

STEVE: Descartes claimed that different mental faculties cannot truly
be thought of as the mind's parts, because it is the *same mind* which
employs itself in willing, desiring, believing, understanding, and so
on. What do you say to that?

MARY: I say that assumes the troublesome picture of the mind as
some kind of enduring unified entity that exists mysteriously
behind the scenes and that observes each mental state as it occurs.
There are good reasons not to think of the mind in such a pecu-
liar way. For one thing, my mind is not something *in addition to* the
sequence of my mental states, but rather is simply the entity that *is
composed of* my mental states. Descartes makes it sound as though
the mind views the sequence of our mental states in the way that
we view segments of film in a continuous movie. But this is difficult
to understand. Your mind is not something extra behind the scenes
passively watching the train of your mental states.

STEVE: I know what you mean; I was just curious how you might respond.

MARY: Anyway, I have trouble overall with Dave's use of the term 'conceive.'

DAVE: How so?

MARY: As even Descartes recognized, the term 'conceive' might mean either 'imagine' or 'understand.' Imagining literally involves 'forming an image of' or 'picturing in one's mind,' whereas understanding is more 'conceptual' and does not require the ability to picture something. So when you say you cannot conceive of your mind as divisible, which do you mean?

DAVE: Why does that matter?

MARY: Because, first, if you mean 'imagine,' then you are in deep trouble.

DAVE: Why?

MARY: You would be implicitly assuming in premise 2 that since you cannot imagine something to be the case, then it could not be the case. Since you cannot imagine your mind as divisible, then your mind cannot be divisible. But inferring *from* the fact that something is unimaginable *to* the fact that it is not the case or not possible is a terrible inference.

I'll give you an example: I cannot imagine or 'picture' a five-hundred-sided figure, but it clearly does not follow that there isn't one, let alone that one is not possible. Of course, I can still 'understand' or 'conceive' what such a figure would be like. Perhaps I could even draw one with the help of an artist. The same goes for imagining a leopard with forty-five spots, picturing two billion dollars in my apartment, being ninety-three million miles away from the sun, and so on.

DAVE: I see. Well then, by 'conceive' I should probably mean something more like 'understand.' If we cannot understand something in the sense that it is conceptually incoherent, like a 'round square,' then it wouldn't be possible. This is the way I think of the term 'conceive' in premise 2. I can't understand predicating 'divisibility' to my mind or my mental states when I introspect.

STEVE: But *we* seem to be able to understand that. Remember Mary's point about thinking of her mind as having parts, and so on. This seems to go against your claim.

MARY: Exactly, Steve.

DAVE: Even if I grant your point here, it wouldn't alter the idea that individual mental states are not divisible, and so the argument could be recast by emphasizing the fact that I cannot conceive of my individual mental states as having parts.

STEVE: But if you do that, then the same seems true about individual physical particles. That is, it is just as difficult to understand that every physical particle is divisible. Many philosophers and physicists believe that ultimately there must be physical particles without parts. So you cannot use the appropriate difference between mental states and all physical stuff in order to prove your conclusion.

DAVE: Perhaps, but, according to your materialism, Mary, wouldn't an individual mental state involve more than a single particle in the brain?

MARY: Of course, but there is another serious problem with the whole way that you approach this issue. It has to do with how you emphasize the first-person or 'introspective' point of view.

DAVE: How do you mean?

MARY: We can learn about our minds by thinking to ourselves, but surely we can also learn many things from a third-person point of view. That is, you can learn things about my mind and I can learn things about your mind through observation. Scientifically speaking, psychiatrists and neuropsychologists can by observation discover quite a bit about the workings of another's mind. Don't you agree?

DAVE: Yes, as long as you are not assuming that the brain is the mind.

MARY: No, but third-person observation is important in the investigation of the mind, isn't it?

DAVE: Again, yes, we can infer things about another's mind on the basis of observation; so what's your point?

MARY: Your method in the Divisibility Argument assumes that the true nature of the mind can be grasped solely through introspection or from the first-person point of view. And this is wrong, as even you seem to agree.

DAVE: How so? And what does this have to do with the Divisibility Argument?

MARY: Even if I grant you that *I* cannot conceive of *my* mind as divided, this would only be so from the first-person perspective. It would not follow that my mind is not really divisible or could not be conceived as such from another's perspective. Even if *I* cannot conceive of *my* mind as divided from *my* point of view, it doesn't follow that *you* cannot understand *my* mind as divided.

STEVE: Right, and also, Dave, you seem to be making a general claim about the nature of all minds, that is, that they all are nonphysical and distinct from their corresponding bodies. You are ultimately not making a claim just about the nature of your own mind. But I don't see what entitles you to make such a general claim.

DAVE: It is difficult to see how anyone could say that someone else's mind is divisible without assuming that materialism is true. Aren't you saying that a scientist can view your brain as having parts and so therefore your mind is divisible?

MARY: No, I don't think I'm assuming materialism. Imagine someone who knows nothing about philosophy or about the brain, and hasn't thought about this issue at all. Doesn't it make sense for him to say to a friend: "There are parts of your mind that are hidden from me," "There are parts of your mind and personality that I don't understand," and so on?

STEVE: Actually, what about multiple personality disorder, which is now called **dissociative identity disorder** or DID for short? Take a severe case where a person, Joe, rarely even realizes that he has the problem. We can and do see Joe's mind as divided even if he doesn't think of himself that way. We learn about Joe's condition through third-person observation and eventually through scientific investigation.

MARY: Good! Right! And we certainly aren't assuming materialism when we make this judgment about Joe's mind. Moreover, this is a clear case where the third-person perspective reveals the true nature of a mind as divided regardless of how it seems from the first-person perspective. So your argument fails here as well.

DAVE: Interesting, but in DID cases I'd be tempted to believe that the subject really has two minds rather than one divided mind. Neither mind is divisible.

MARY: Really?

DAVE: Yes. Think about something we often say: "He is an entirely different person from yesterday." If, as seems obvious, different people have different minds, then we should say that two different minds are associated with Joe's body.

MARY: But surely such talk is merely metaphorical; we don't mean literally that such a person really has two distinct minds.

DAVE: Perhaps. I'm not sure though.

STEVE: Oh, come on! You do see the obvious problems: If Joe has two minds, why don't we all "really" have two or more minds? If Joe really has two minds, then which one does the name 'Joe' refer to? If a DID patient has five personalities, then does he or she have five minds?

MARY: And how about the less dramatic example of an amnesia victim? Isn't it literally true to say that some parts of that person's mind are hidden from him and from us?

DAVE: Let me think about that one. But I understand that some well-respected philosophers and psychologists agree with me on the question of two minds.

MARY: But don't they usually have materialist reasons for their position? For example, reasons which have to do with the two hemispheres in the brain?

DAVE: Sometimes. I'll have to find out.

STEVE: Actually, Mary, let Dave off the hook on this one because I'm eager to hear his other favorite argument for dualism. You said earlier that the Divisibility Argument was only one of two.

1.4 The Argument from Introspection

DAVE: Yes. Here it is (*Dave writes the following argument down*):

(1) Mental states are knowable through introspection.
(2) Brain states are *not* knowable through introspection.
Therefore, (3) mental states are not brain states.

Let's call this the Argument from Introspection. It also relies on Leibniz's Law and uses a different property to prove the distinctness of brain states and mental states: the property of being knowable through introspection. In this case, the mind has the property and the brain lacks it. I can know about my feelings and thoughts by introspection, but clearly I cannot learn anything about my brain through introspection. So my mental states cannot *be* my brain states. After all, humans were around a long time before we knew anything about our brains, but it would be ridiculous to say that we didn't know anything about our minds during that time.

STEVE: Can you give a particular example?

DAVE: Sure. Right now I have a desire for another drink. I know that I have that mental state simply by examining my own mind and without knowing anything about what might "correspond" to it in terms of brain activity. Thus, my desire cannot simply *be* the brain process.

MARY: *First* of all, I think you are making a mistake similar to the one you made earlier in that you rely heavily on introspection.

DAVE: How so?

MARY: Before I explain, let me give an analogy with our perception of outer objects. When we look at a physical object, do we perceive its true nature?

DAVE: I suppose not if you mean in the scientific sense of ultimate particles, not to mention the difficult issue of color. We learn about the object's true physical makeup through scientific investigation.

MARY: And there is of course a very good reason why we are not built to perceive the world in that way.

STEVE: I'd say. It would be very confusing if all we perceived were atoms whizzing around. Our species wouldn't have survived.

MARY: Right. And so why shouldn't the same go for mental states, which are, we might say, the objects of *inner* perception?

DAVE: How do you mean?

MARY: Well, you perceive your desire for a drink via introspection, but there is no reason to suppose that its true nature is revealed that way. When we perceive the table we do not perceive its true nature without further scientific study. But this doesn't mean that the table is entirely distinct from the atoms that compose it, right?

DAVE: Right.

MARY: So, similarly, just because you don't perceive your desire *as a brain state*, it doesn't follow that it is distinct from your brain. In other words, the Argument from Introspection fails to prove that mental states are distinct from brain states. It's merely that we cannot learn about any identity through introspection. But ignorance about the true nature of mental states cannot be used as an argument for dualism.

STEVE: Right, and just as before with outer objects, that's what we should expect because it would be ridiculous if we did seem to introspect electrochemical reactions when we focused our attention on our mental states. Talk about confusing! We are fortunately aware of our mental states only *as mental states* and not *as brain states*, but it doesn't follow that they are distinct. Objects are not always really the way they appear and this goes as much for inner mental states as it does for outer reality.

Dave: I suppose so, but at most you've only shown that mental states *could* be brain states, nothing stronger.

Mary: But that's all I need for now. My aim here has only been to refute the Argument from Introspection. Other independent support for materialism has already been given. But, anyway, there is a *second* and more serious objection to your argument.

Dave: What's that?

Mary: It has to do with your application of Leibniz's Law. I have recently learned that the law cannot be used in contexts like this one.

Dave: What kinds of contexts?

Mary: Leibniz's Law fails in what are called **intensional contexts**; that is, cases where replacing one co-referring term with another can change a statement's truth-value.

Steve: I'm not sure I follow.

Mary: Let me explain. Remember how two different expressions or terms can refer to the same object?

Steve: Yes, like 'heat' and 'mean molecular kinetic energy,' or 'Babe Ruth' and 'the first baseball player to hit sixty home runs in a season,' or 'water' and 'H_2O.'

Mary: Right. These are called 'co-referring' terms or expressions.

Dave: So?

Mary: Normally when one of the expressions is replaced by the other in a sentence, the new sentence retains the same truth-value. That is, if the first sentence was false, then it remains false; if it was true, it stays true.

DAVE: OK. So, for example, the following sentence is true:

(1) Babe Ruth played most of his career for the New York Yankees.

Now replace 'Babe Ruth' with the other expression and we get:

(2) The first baseball player to hit sixty home runs in a season played most of his career for the New York Yankees.

Sentence (2) is also true. I can see how these can be generated *ad infinitum*.

STEVE: Me too, and this is also true for false sentences remaining false after the substitution of a co-referring expression. For example, it is false that "Babe Ruth weighed 140 pounds in his last playing year"; and so it remains false that "The first baseball player to hit sixty home runs in a season weighed 140 pounds in his last playing year."

MARY: Right! And these are the kinds of cases where Leibniz's Law *can be* used. That is, we would expect to find any property true of Babe Ruth to be true of the first player to hit sixty home runs, and anything false to remain false. Suppose you were reading a history book and you wondered whether two of the characters mentioned were really the same person even though two different names had been used. In order to show non-identity, all you needed was to find a single property that one had and the other lacked.

DAVE: Yes, and that's what I've done in the Argument from Introspection.

MARY: But the problem is that in some contexts the truth-value will change after the substitution, and so Leibniz's Law cannot be used to prove non-identity. One such context involves sentences with mental expressions like 'believes that,' 'conceives that,' 'thinks that,' 'knows that,' and so on. Otherwise, we could prove the non-identity of *anything* that has two names or expressions for it.

DAVE: Can you give an example?

MARY: Sure. My sister Margaret knows very little about baseball, but does know that Babe Ruth played primarily for the Yankees.

Margaret knows that he was a great player but knows few, if any, statistics. Take the sentence:

(3) Margaret knows that Babe Ruth played most of his career for the Yankees.

This statement is true, but now make the substitution, and we have the following *false* sentence:

(4) Margaret knows that the first player to hit sixty home runs in a season played most of his career for the Yankees.

DAVE: Interesting. Yeah, we wouldn't say that she knew about the sixty home run season.

STEVE: Here's another one: My four-year-old niece, Cathy, knows nothing about chemistry, but knows what water is. The following is true:

(5) Cathy knows that her pool is filled with water.

But it is false that:

(6) Cathy knows that her pool is filled with H_2O.

DAVE: I see, but what does all this have to do with the Argument from Introspection?

MARY: I'm getting there. But do you see how if we used Leibniz's Law in this context we could, for example, absurdly prove that water is not identical with H_2O?

DAVE: I think so, but explain.

STEVE: Let me give it a try.

MARY: OK.

STEVE: Water has a property which H_2O lacks, namely, "known by Cathy to be in her pool." Therefore, by Leibniz's Law, water is not identical with H_2O.

MARY: Do you see how the same problem always haunts Leibniz's Law in these contexts?

DAVE: I guess so.

MARY: The problem with the Argument from Introspection is that it applies Leibniz's Law where it shouldn't: in an intensional context. So you have not proven that mental states are distinct from brain states any more than we have just shown water to be distinct from H_2O. Just as Cathy is ignorant of H_2O and has to learn about its identity with water through science, so are we often ignorant about which brain states correspond to our mental states. But we can learn about them through the scientific discipline known as neurophysiology. In neither case, however, is any non-identity shown. You can't use properties like 'knowable through introspection' to show non-identity.

STEVE: Right. And again, if Leibniz's Law could be used in such contexts, then we could show non-identity in any situation. All we'd have to do is find someone who knows, thinks, or believes one thing about an object while being ignorant about some other aspect of it.

MARY: So my current desire to have another drink can still be identical with one of my brain processes, even though I couldn't know it through introspection.

DAVE: I see the problem. Perhaps it is insurmountable, but you talk as if you do know that mental states are brain states.

MARY: I think I do based on the evidence and reason. At the least, it seems like a much more rational belief than substance dualism.

STEVE: But isn't Dave right, Mary, to question your optimism about materialism? You speak of "correlations" between mental states and brain processes. That seems rather weak as evidence for materialism.

MARY: I disagree. You have to take it as only one piece of evidence for materialism, along with evolution and the other considerations I had discussed with Dave before you came.

STEVE: I know what you mean. Remember, we also talked about it last week.

MARY: Yes, I remember. You must admit that we have a good deal of knowledge about the way neurons work and how some brain activity is correlated with certain types of mental states. For example, many parts of the brain are clearly linked to emotions, memories, visual experiences, auditory perceptions, and so on.

DAVE: I am not sure what these correlations prove about the nature of the mind. Anyway, neuroscientists don't have a clue about most higher-order cognitive functioning.

MARY: Again, I'm not saying we have all the answers now. But at least we're progressing and learning more and more every day. On the other hand, if you are right, Dave, then we couldn't scientifically learn anything about the mind, since it is not physical and therefore could not be the object of any scientific investigation.

DAVE: Well, first, I have nothing against scientifically examining and learning about the brain. It's no doubt a very important part of the body. But I don't believe that my mind *is* my brain, or that my current desire for another drink and my love for my wife *just are* some electrochemical processes in my brain. Second, I don't share your apparent desire to restrict reality to the physical.

MARY: I'm not arbitrarily restricting anything. I am not in principle opposed to the existence of nonphysical things, but I fail to see the basis for believing in nonphysical minds in this particular case. Actually, I do believe in other nonphysical entities.

STEVE: Like what? Not God, right? That's what you told me the other day.

MARY: I don't believe in God, but I believe that numbers are nonphysical entities.

STEVE: Why?

MARY: Well, for example, we couldn't go find the number 5 itself and destroy it. Even if a mad scientist found a way to destroy every instance of 5, would the number *itself* have gone out of existence?

STEVE: No.

MARY: And if the existing 5's were all destroyed, would the first person who wrote the number '5' have created it anew?

STEVE: No, so I suppose the number 5 itself and all other numbers have always existed and always will. Numbers are nonphysical and eternal.

MARY: There are certainly some numbers which have never been written down anywhere. Don't they exist now? Of course. Would they only come into existence after they were written down? No. I agree that numbers are nonphysical and eternal.

DAVE: I'm glad to hear you say that, so why don't you give nonphysical minds the same due?

MARY: Because I don't have any reason to. Besides, there are other serious problems with substance dualism that we haven't discussed yet.

DAVE: Like what?

MARY: Let's meet again tomorrow. All this talk about a desire for another drink has made me thirsty. Let's go play some pool and talk about something else.

STEVE: Sounds good. I'm starting to lose my mind or brain or whatever.

DAVE: Me too.

THE SECOND NIGHT

2.1 Substance Dualism and Interactionism

MARY: Hi, Steve. You're right on time.

STEVE: Hello, Mary. Where's Dave?

MARY: He should be here soon.

STEVE: Here he comes.

MARY: How are you doing, Dave? Are you ready for more of this?

DAVE: You bet. But where did we leave off last night?

STEVE: I remember. Mary was saying that she had other serious objections to substance dualism.

DAVE: Well, fire away, Mary.

STEVE: And I have some real problems with dualism regarding the interaction between the mind and the body. But go ahead, Mary.

MARY: Actually, my main problem with substance dualism is similar.

DAVE: Well?

MARY: Let me first explain another obvious advantage of materialism and then get to the objection to dualism. First, Dave, you do agree that mental states causally interact with the body or the brain, and vice versa?

DAVE: Of course, and virtually all substance dualists agree. This dualist position is called **interactionism**.

MARY: For example, if I kick you in the leg, Dave, eventually you'll experience a mental state of pain and probably anger. Your pain, in turn, might cause your heart to beat faster, or might even cause you to kick me in return.

STEVE: Yeah, a desire for a drink will cause my body to move to buy a beer. Conversely, our bodily changes can cause mental changes, which can sometimes be very damaging. The examples could go on forever.

MARY: There is no conceptual bar to materialism explaining such causal interaction between the mind and body or brain. I'm not say-ing that we know all of the details yet, but we do know a lot about how the nervous system and brain work. So, for example, kicking you in the leg causes damage to a particular area and the nerves cause an impulse and message to travel up through the spinal col-umn. Ultimately, the impulse will reach an area of the brain, and the final neural firing in the sequence *is* the pain you feel. Conversely, we know how some mental states, such as anger, cause bodily changes and certain bodily movements.

DAVE: I mostly agree, but I must disagree with your *identification* of the pain and the neural firing.

MARY: But my point here is that materialism at least has the potential to explain the obvious causation which occurs between the mind and the body. Since the mind is literally part of the body, then there is nothing inherently bizarre about such interaction. There is causation within the physical world, and now it's up to us to explain it the best we can through further scientific investigation.

DAVE: But I do not think that the pain or anger *just is* one of the brain states in the chain of causes. Mental states are not physical; they occur within our nonphysical minds.

STEVE: I think Mary's point is that materialism at least has a chance at explaining the causal interaction between the mind and the body, whereas dualism has none. Therefore, we should accept the more explanatorily useful theory.

MARY: Exactly.

DAVE: But what's your specific objection?

STEVE: Well, there are several major objections to interactionism as far as I know. *One* has to do with the general problem of explaining how physical events can cause events in a nonphysical mind, and vice versa. First of all, one side of the causal interaction will always be unobservable, so how could any dualist explanation be forthcoming?

MARY: Dave, take my example from earlier. I kick you in the leg and you then must acknowledge the physical facts about what happens up through the nervous system and into the brain. But instead of simply admitting that the last neural firing in the causal sequence *just is* the pain you feel, you think that the last neural firing *causes* the further pain state in your nonphysical mind.

DAVE: Right. The mental state is not identical with the neural state, but rather is caused by it.

MARY: But *how* in the world does that happen?

DAVE: I don't know, but that doesn't mean it doesn't happen that way.

STEVE: Doesn't that bother you, Dave? Why believe that causation could even exist between such radically different substances?

DAVE: I don't have the answer, but neither do you.

MARY: Sure, but at least we have a chance to explain mental-physical interaction. If dualism were true, then it would be impossible to explain or understand it. Doesn't that bother you?

DAVE: Sometimes, but again I obviously don't share your craving to have everything explained by science. We also all know how often science has been mistaken in the past, and I don't see why I should become a materialist just because materialism seems more consistent with science.

STEVE: Actually, it's possible that science, and especially neurophysiology, could go some way toward resolving the issue between dualism and materialism. That is, there's a possible experiment that could help to determine which view is right.

MARY: Really? What?

STEVE: We've been talking about brain states causing mental states. Let's look at it the other way around. Dualism also has the converse problem: How do nonphysical mental events cause brain changes and eventually bodily movements?

MARY: Of course.

STEVE: So now if dualism were true, we should expect to see neurons regularly firing *without any physical cause*. Right?

DAVE: I'm not sure I follow.

STEVE: Well, according to materialism, the brain is a closed physical system, and we know from neurology how neurons cause each other to fire. I'll skip over the details here. If materialism is true, then whenever a neuron fires, the cause must be some other physical or neural state.

DAVE: Right.

STEVE: But if dualism is true, neural activity must often be caused by nonphysical mental events. Right?

DAVE: Sure, I suppose so.

STEVE: But there has never been any evidence to suggest that this is so. That is, we don't find neurons regularly firing without any other physical cause. So interactionist dualism must be false.

DAVE: Are you sure there is no evidence favoring the dualist?

STEVE: Not as far as I know.

DAVE: Now that you mention it, I thought I heard one of the other graduate students say that he knows of a few scientists who are dualists for this very reason. I wasn't sure what he meant then, but now I see the point. That is, perhaps the jury is at least still out in the scientific community regarding the evidence.

MARY: Really? I'd be interested in learning more about this, but I'd be shocked to learn that neurons fired regularly without any physical cause. However, I agree that *if* this were so, then that would be good evidence, and even scientific evidence, for substance dualism.

STEVE: Maybe we should look into this a bit more. But I am still baffled about exactly *how* any dualist interaction could take place and that's one reason why I often lean toward materialism.

DAVE: What's the other reason? You said earlier you had two.

STEVE: Right. The *second* serious problem has to do with the apparent fact that dualist interactionism is inconsistent with the well-established scientific **Conservation of Energy Principle**, which says that the total amount of energy in the universe, or any controlled part of it, remains constant. So any loss of energy in a cause must be passed on as a corresponding gain of energy in the effect. The cue ball loses energy when it hits another ball, but the energy doesn't magically disappear and go out of existence; it's passed on to the other ball. In general, then, energy is neither created nor destroyed.

DAVE: So where's the inconsistency?

STEVE: Interactionism claims that there is causation between the physical world and the nonphysical mental realm.

DAVE: Yes.

STEVE: But since minds wouldn't be part of the physical world, there would then be sudden gains and losses in the amount of total energy whenever mental events caused physical events, or vice versa. That is, when a physical event caused a mental event, energy would literally go out of the physical world, since causation involves a transfer of energy from cause to effect. Conversely, when a mental event caused a physical event, there would have to be a gain of energy in the physical world.

MARY: Yes. This seems like a serious problem for you, Dave. Clearly there is no scientific evidence of such a bizarre phenomenon.

DAVE: Well, have controlled experiments been performed using thinking people enclosed in an area in order to determine whether there are any such gains or losses?

MARY: I'm not sure, but I doubt it. These experiments wouldn't be so easy to perform because it would be difficult for physicists to measure what would have to be very small violations of the principle. But even assuming that they can be performed accurately, you can't believe that such losses or gains would actually occur.

DAVE: Maybe they would. For someone who relies so heavily on science, Mary, you really aren't sure about many potentially important scientific experiments.

MARY: But the fact remains that dualism is inconsistent with the Conservation of Energy Principle. One says that the amount of energy remains constant and the other entails that there are losses and gains of energy. If we made a graph with "amount of energy" on the vertical and "time" on the horizontal, the Conservation Principle would yield a straight line across. Where it began on the horizontal line would depend on which enclosed portion of the world is measured. On the other hand, substance dualism would yield a line going across and often up and down, with the amount of energy varying whenever mental-physical causation occurred. Clearly both can't be true, and, given a choice between them, why would anyone opt for dualism?

STEVE: I certainly wouldn't.

DAVE: Well, maybe the Conservation of Energy Principle isn't true or is only true concerning purely physical objects without minds.

MARY: Are you serious? The principle is true everywhere in the entire universe, including among all other animals, but then does *not* apply *only* when humans are involved? Incredible!

DAVE: Maybe, but I'm simply not as inclined to treat the principle as so certain. For one thing, it's obviously an inductive generalization from a relatively small sample of experiments. Clearly, astronomers and physicists can't be certain that it holds everywhere in the entire vast universe.

MARY: Well, what can I say? I still don't see why anyone would give more weight to dualism.

DAVE: OK, but there may be other possible explanations consistent with dualism.

STEVE: Such as?

DAVE: You mentioned the "transfer of energy from cause to effect," and you have simply assumed it in your argument.

STEVE: Of course; that's the way it works.

DAVE: No, that's the way it works *as far as we know in the physical world*. Maybe it doesn't always work that way. Or maybe causation between the physical and the nonphysical doesn't involve a transfer of energy in the same way. After all, you'd expect it to be a bit different; wouldn't you? So even if the level of energy does remain constant, as the Conservation Principle says, that may not really contradict interactionism. You must remember that it's a principle of *physics*, which means that it may apply only in the physical world. Things may work quite differently with mental-physical interaction.

STEVE: It's possible I guess.

DAVE: And if the term 'energy' is defined in the usual way as a physical constant—the 'e' for energy in physics—then I'm not even sure if it makes sense to talk about energy going in and out of the physical universe. The term 'energy' as applied to nonphysical minds would either be meaningless or it would have to mean something else.

MARY: That's a good point, Dave. I'd have to think about that some more.

2.2 Brain Damage and an Afterlife

STEVE: But, Dave, don't you think that brain damage causing mental defects refutes dualism and therefore favors materialism?

DAVE: No. Why?

STEVE: You can also think of it as a *third* objection to substance dualism. Well, we do know that damage to certain specific brain areas causes specific mental problems, for example, memory loss, visual and hearing problems, and language comprehension disorders. For example, cortical blindness is a loss of vision resulting from damage to areas of the visual cortex. Cortical deafness is a loss of hearing or the ability to recognize sounds, including speech, resulting from damage to regions of the auditory cortex in the temporal lobes. Damage to no other brain areas results in such specific visual and auditory deficits.

MARY: I've also recently read about other disorders. There are so many of them and some are very strange. There is always a brain lesion or abnormality present in such cases. There's something called **agnosia**, which is a loss of ability to recognize objects, persons, sounds, shapes, or smells even while the specific sense itself is not defective. For example, a patient with visual agnosia will be unable to name or recognize a whistle. Associative agnosics are not blind and do not have damage to the relevant areas of the visual cortex. **Prosopagnosia** is the inability to recognize familiar faces, typically caused by damage to the fusiform gyrus in the occipito-temporal cortex.

DAVE: Very odd indeed.

STEVE: And **somatoparaphrenia** is a bizarre body delusion where one denies ownership of a limb or an entire side of one's body. You know like saying "this is not my leg" (*Mary grabs her own left leg*). It is a "depersonalization disorder" and is usually caused by extensive right hemisphere lesions. Doesn't it follow that those brain areas just *were* where the mental states occurred? That is, doesn't such evidence show materialism to be true, and therefore dualism false?

DAVE: Not really.

STEVE: Why?

DAVE: Because if you damage or eliminate a cause, then you damage or eliminate the effect.

MARY: How do you mean?

DAVE: You recall that interactionism acknowledges, for example, that brain events cause mental events.

MARY: Sure, and you deny that the brain event (BE) *is* the mental event (ME).

DAVE: Well, brain damage cannot show dualism to be false, because if part of the causal sequence of events to one's nonphysical mind is disturbed or damaged, then we should expect there to be a corresponding problem in the mind. I claim that "BE causes ME," whereas you insist that "BE = ME." But in either case damage to the brain area will result in damage to the correlated mental state. Obviously, if materialism is true, then damage to the brain area will result in damage to the mind because you believe that the BEs *are* MEs.

MARY: Right.

DAVE: But interactionism can equally well explain this phenomenon. If BE causes ME, then, when the relevant brain area is damaged, the corresponding part of the mind is also disturbed, because the cause of ME has been disturbed or destroyed. So you can't use brain damage to refute interactionism or to support materialism. If, for example, there is damage to the brain area which typically *causes* conscious visual experiences, then I can just as easily explain why the person's visual capacities have been damaged.

STEVE: Interesting, but surely that's not the more natural or simple explanation. Plus, I thought you were telling us last night that the mind doesn't have "parts."

MARY: Good point, Steve. I agree and, Dave, I'm not so sure that your reply really helps you in the end anyway. For example, doesn't it cause trouble in terms of your belief in immortality?

DAVE: How so?

MARY: Well, take the case where brain damage causes the destruction or elimination of a conscious mental capacity.

DAVE: Yes.

MARY: Now, what happens to the brain upon bodily death?

STEVE: The entire brain ceases to function and is ultimately destroyed through decomposition.

DAVE: Right.

MARY: Well, by your own reasoning, Dave, interactionism would have to admit that when the brain is eliminated or destroyed, the mind is also eliminated or destroyed. That is, the cause of your mind is destroyed and therefore so is the effect. Thus, there couldn't be immortality because one's mind would cease to exist upon brain death. So what is the point of your reply here if it undermines your belief in immortality? I mean, that's how we started all this last night. Remember?

DAVE: Sure, but I'm not convinced that my belief in immortality is seriously threatened.

MARY: Why not? You might still *want to* believe that your mind is a nonphysical substance distinct from your body, but if it causally depends for its existence on the proper functioning of your brain, then there can't be any immortality.

STEVE: Interesting point. Isn't this a serious problem for you, Dave?

DAVE: Perhaps, but maybe the mind only causally depends on the brain during the time our bodies are functioning on earth. And then, after bodily death, one's mind no longer needs one's brain to function properly.

STEVE: I'm not convinced by that, Dave. It really sounds rather arbitrary to concede that your mind depends on your brain up until bodily death, but then to claim that it suddenly doesn't depend on anything else after that point.

MARY: Sounds weak and arbitrary to me, too. Also, what happens to those destroyed conscious capacities upon bodily death?

DAVE: What do you mean?

MARY: Well, suppose you have severe amnesia during the last few years of your life caused by brain damage. Wouldn't that mental damage then carry over to your "afterlife"? We can put it in terms of a dilemma:
If so, then the mind's causal dependence on the brain has some very serious and disturbing consequences for the quality of one's afterlife. Even if your mind is able to survive brain death, what kind of mind would it be?
On the other hand, *if* any or all mental damage does *not* carry over to the afterlife, then you really need to explain how the mental damage one suffers during life on earth magically disappears upon bodily death. I mean, how is all this mental functioning suddenly recovered or restored?

DAVE: I see the dilemma. I'll need to think about that one, but remember from last night the possibility of God restoring our memories or minds in some way?

MARY: Oh my goodness, let's not go back to that again.

2.3 Parallelism and Epiphenomenalism

STEVE: Perhaps there are other versions of dualism that can avoid some of Dave's problems.

DAVE: Well, actually, there is even another type of substance dualism that has the one advantage of avoiding most of the problems facing interactionism.

STEVE: What is it?

DAVE: It's called **parallelism**. It is a form of substance dualism because it holds that the mind is a nonphysical substance distinct from the body. But it denies that the two causally interact, and therefore, it avoids the problems that stem from any alleged mind-body causal interaction.

STEVE: But what does parallelism say about the mind-body relationship? Surely it must give some explanation.

DAVE: Yes, parallelism says that mental events and bodily events are correlated, but that there is no interaction between the mental and physical realms. So physical events cause other physical events, and mental events cause other mental events.

STEVE: In other words, my mental realm runs parallel to the sequence of my bodily, and especially brain, events in some kind of perfect synchrony or harmony.

DAVE: Right. The idea is that the mental and physical realms operate along parallel tracks, always in perfect harmony. So, for example, when I kick you in the leg and then you feel pain, there is no causation between those events, but rather your mental "track" is such that you feel the pain at about the same time as the physical bodily event occurs. And the same type of answer goes for other familiar examples of alleged mind-body interaction.

STEVE: So, I have a mental sequence of events and a bodily sequence of events running in parallel to each other without any causal interaction at all between them?

DAVE: Yes. Think of it as follows (*Dave writes on a piece of paper*):

$$ME_1 \rightarrow ME_2 \rightarrow ME_3 \rightarrow ME_4 \rightarrow ME_5 \rightarrow ME_6 \text{ and so on.}$$
$$BE_1 \rightarrow BE_2 \rightarrow BE_3 \rightarrow BE_4 \rightarrow BE_5 \rightarrow BE_6 \text{ and so on.}$$

Let's use the "arrow" symbol to indicate a causal sequence as follows: Bodily Event$_1$ causes Bodily Event$_2$ and so on. Mental Event$_1$ causes, or at least just precedes, Mental Event$_2$ and so on. But there is no causation going from the mental to the physical, or vice versa. BE_1 might be the leg damage or injury from my kick and ME1 might be the pain you feel. They occur almost simultaneously, but BE_1

doesn't cause ME_1. This is obviously very different from interactionism, which would frequently have arrows going from MEs to BEs, and vice versa.

MARY: Oh yeah. I think Leibniz used the analogy of two clocks or watches that are in perfect "preestablished harmony." They have been constructed in such a way that their subsequent agreement is guaranteed. Think of the mind and body this way. That is, they reliably correspond to each other in the way that perfectly synchronized clocks correspond. Minds follow their own laws of development and bodies follow the laws of physics and motion.

STEVE: I see. Granted that this alternative form of dualism avoids the problems with interactionism, doesn't it suffer from other and even more serious difficulties?

DAVE: I think so. That's why I opt for interactionism.

STEVE: Why exactly aren't you a parallelist instead?

DAVE: My main reason is simply that I don't wish to deny the apparently obvious fact that mental events cause bodily events, and vice versa. Remember all of the examples we used earlier?

STEVE: Sure.

DAVE: I mean, the parallelist seems committed to holding that statements like "your kick to my leg caused my pain" are literally false. I can't accept that. Just think of all of the false statements we'd be making all the time. I prefer not to stray so far from common sense.

STEVE: I see. Statements like "my looking at the fire truck caused me to have a red visual experience"; "my eating the spaghetti caused me to have a certain taste sensation"; "my desire for a drink caused me to move toward the bar"; and "you talking to me caused me to have certain auditory sensations" would all literally be false according to parallelism.

DAVE: Yes, because there really is no mental-physical interaction at all. That's a bit too much for me to swallow.

MARY: Parallelism does sound very counterintuitive when you put it that way. Of course, we can agree that physical events cause other physical events. And we can agree that mental events *sometimes* cause other mental events, such as my thought about the escaped convict causes me to have a fear for my life. But to deny all mind-body interaction seems extreme. And, also, why does the synchrony even hold between the mental and the physical?

DAVE: Well, the answer will likely come with the help of the clock analogy.

MARY: OK, but who or what sets our mental and physical clocks so that they always run perfectly together? What prevents the "tracks" from getting "out of synch" and sometimes looking like this? (*she scribbles quickly on paper*):

$$ME_5 \rightarrow ME_6 \rightarrow ME_7 \rightarrow ME_8$$
$$BE_5 \rightarrow BE_6 \rightarrow BE_7 \rightarrow BE_8 \rightarrow BE_9?$$

DAVE: The parallelist will probably say that the only answer is God. Only God could have the knowledge and power to engineer things so perfectly. God sets our mental and body clocks to work in harmony. Otherwise, for example, I might sometimes feel the pain in my leg *before* you kick me. To be fair, Leibniz, for example, probably thought that he had already shown that God exists. So, he felt justified in using God as a creator to answer this sort of worry.

MARY: Well, I can't believe that a dualist must embrace theism in order to defend her solution to the mind-body problem, especially after our conversation early last night. Here we have a dualist view that can help us to understand the possibility of immortality, but in order to handle a very basic objection about mental-physical causal interaction, it *must* assume that God exists. That type of reasoning is not very convincing to me.

STEVE: I agree, but there would be another serious and more hypothetical objection to parallelism even on the assumption that God exists.

MARY: What's that?

STEVE: Well, suppose that God suddenly decided to destroy all human minds. If parallelism were true, then what would change in the physical world?

DAVE: Absolutely nothing.

STEVE: Right, but surely this is a very bizarre consequence of any theory of mind.

MARY: Sure. If God destroyed all minds today, it would have no effect on the movements of human bodies tomorrow. We wouldn't have any thoughts, feelings, and so on, but we would still go to our classes, write papers, eat meals, have conversations, and so on. All human physical behavior and interaction would continue in the same way despite the lack of any minds.

DAVE: Yeah, because if parallelism is true, minds have no causal bearing on or relevance to what happens in the physical world. All of our physical behavior would proceed unchanged despite the lack of any mentality behind it.

MARY: So the ultimate point seems to be that, contrary to parallelism, we really do believe that there is mind-body causal interaction. Right?

DAVE: Yes, and that's why I much prefer interactionism despite its own problems.

STEVE: I see, and there is the alternative, middle ground dualist position called **epiphenomenalism**, which says that mental events are caused by, but not reducible to, brain events such that mental events are mere epiphenomena. Mental states or events are caused by physical states or events in the brain, but they do *not* themselves cause anything. The causal direction of arrows goes only one way, from BEs to MEs. Our conscious lives are, we might say, just "along for the ride."

DAVE: Right, it again *seems* as if our mental life affects our body and the physical world surrounding us: it *seems* that fear makes our heart beat faster. In reality, however, the causal sequence of events leading to the increased heartbeat is not fear, but the state of our nervous system which causes the fear and increased heart rate. So, we can at least be assured that all physical events are caused by other physical events with some physical events also causing mental events.

MARY: I think Thomas Huxley used this analogy: the relationship between mind and brain is like the relationship between the steam whistle that accompanies the work of a locomotive engine. Just as the steam whistle is caused by the engine's operations, but has no causal influence upon it, so too the mental is caused by neural mechanisms, but in turn has no causal influence on anything physical.

STEVE: That's right, Mary.

DAVE: But, again, the obvious initial objection is that this is incredibly counterintuitive, for whatever that is worth. What could be more obvious from the first-person point of view than that my pain makes me cry or that the visual experience of the charging lion makes me run away? At the very least, the epiphenomenalist, like the parallelist, also owes us an explanation of the *appearance* of interaction. Why does it appear as though my pain causes me to cry? I don't think epiphenomenalists are likely to turn to God for an explanation.

MARY: Right. Also, if conscious mental states really cause nothing, then there is no reason why they should have evolved. If conscious states clearly modify our behavior in certain ways, then they should be very useful from an evolutionary perspective. So I'd start to wonder why consciousness evolved at all.

STEVE: Interesting. It also doesn't support a belief in an afterlife if you still think that matters.

DAVE: Why?

STEVE: Because mental events still *depend on* brain activity. Once brain activity ceases so would all mental activity.

DAVE: I see; well, that's another reason to reject epiphenomenalism as far as I'm concerned.

MARY: I thought you might say that.

2.4 Type vs. Token Materialism

DAVE: Anyway, we've obviously reached the end of this discussion. I want to get clearer about your materialism, Mary. Your view is not without its own problems, you know.

STEVE: Yeah, good idea. Even though I sometimes lean toward materialism, I have a difficult time with certain aspects of it. That's why I hesitate to so openly declare myself a materialist. Let's put Mary on the spot.

MARY: Fine. What do you want to know?

DAVE: First of all, I'm not quite clear about your view. I understood what you said before, but you talk about "correlations" and "identities" in an often confusing way.

MARY: I hold that every mental state is a physical state or, more specifically, a neural state or brain process.

STEVE: But when you say 'is,' do you mean 'is identical with'?

MARY: Of course. There aren't two different events, but merely two different names or descriptions for one brain event. Remember our discussion last night about co-referring terms?

STEVE: Yes, but can you give an example?

MARY: Sure. My current desire to drink some water is identical with some neural state or event in my brain. Of course I do not know exactly which neural event, but let's call whatever it is 'NE_{100}.' It's the job of neuroscience to correlate mental states with brain states so that we can better discover the identities. We already have some idea about certain types of mental states, such as pain, emotions, memories, and visual experiences. Others will require more investigation, such as particular thoughts and complex higher-order cognitive capacities. But I am confident that we will eventually discover all of the relevant brain state correlations.

STEVE: I'm not that confident. Plus, mere "correlations" can only be the first step to show "identity."

MARY: Sure, but we have many analogous examples from the history of science. People knew about heat and water long before their scientific identity or explanation was discovered. The same goes for 'my desire to drink some water' and any mental state.

STEVE: But are you identifying events or properties?

MARY: How do you mean?

STEVE: Well, the *property* 'being water' is identified with the *property* 'being composed of H_2O.' This entails that anything that is water must be composed of H_2O. If something is not composed of H_2O, then it's not water. Is this what you mean to identify in the mind-brain case, i.e., the properties 'having a desire for water' and 'having NE_{100}'?

MARY: Are you referring to what's called **'type-type' materialism** or **'type-type' identity theory**?

STEVE: Yes.

DAVE: Wait, what's that?

STEVE: As I said, it identifies mental types or properties with brain types or properties.

DAVE: So you are using the terms 'type' and 'property' interchangeably?

STEVE: Yes, pretty much.

MARY: I'm not quite sure yet if I am a type-materialist although some philosophers of mind do hold this position.

DAVE: Why not?

MARY: Unlike the water and H_2O analogy, it seems possible for there to be conscious creatures who can have the desire to drink water, but who do *not* have NE_{100}. For example, if there are conscious beings on other planets, as seems likely, they certainly wouldn't have the same kinds of brains that we do. They probably wouldn't have what we call 'neurons' at all. But I don't want to say that they *couldn't* have the desire to drink water unless they also have NE_{100}. As a matter of fact, the brains of some animals on earth are perhaps different enough from ours so that even they will have different neural processes when they have such a desire. Mental states have what is often called **multiple realizability**, that is, the same mental type can be had by radically different creatures with very different physiologies. Type-materialism seems unwisely to rule this out.

DAVE: I see. Isn't this a very serious problem?

MARY: Many philosophers think so, and that's why many shy away from identifying mental types with specific physical types. It seems too strong in a sense.

STEVE: So you don't necessarily think that mental properties are identical with properties of human-like brains. Are you therefore a **'token-token' identity theorist**?

MARY: I guess so.

DAVE: And what's token-token identity theory?

MARY: Well, it simply equates mental *events* with brain *events*. Events are particulars such as a particular brain process or event inside someone's head.

DAVE: So now you are using 'token' and 'event' interchangeably?

MARY: Sure, although 'state' or 'process' is similar enough. The idea is that any creature's mental state at $time_1$ is simply some physical or brain event *in that creature* at $time_1$. Every mental event is a physical event. You see how this avoids the multiple realizability problem facing the type-materialist.

DAVE: I think so, but tell me anyway.

MARY: My current desire to drink water is identical with NE_{100}, which is some current physical event *in me*. But this does not rule out others having that type of mental state even if they don't have NE_{100}. Some alien creature can still have that same kind of desire, which, given its radically different physiology, wouldn't be identical with NE_{100}. But all the token-materialist claims is that the desire must be identical with one of *its* inner brain-like events, and similarly for any mental state.

STEVE: But token-identity has sometimes been criticized for not being metaphysically robust enough since it wouldn't identify a physical counterpart to mental-state types. Token-token identities aren't general enough for the purpose of scientific explanations. One appeal of type-identity theory is that it gives us generalizations like the ones we find in chemistry. Water is *always* H_2O. So we can actually do science with this knowledge and arrive at general laws of nature.

MARY: Good point so maybe type-identity isn't so bad after all. Maybe the physical type in type-identity theory can at least vary to some extent from species to species. I may have to rethink this.

STEVE: I guess it's not quite that simple then.

MARY: Well, no. And others focus more on the connection to the typical input and the typical output or behavior associated with mental states. Did you want to discuss that as well?

STEVE: Sure, and you know there's a theory called **functionalism** which says that mental states should only be identified with the functional role they play within an organism rather than what physically makes them up. Mental states are analogous to the function of the heart pumping blood throughout the body. It doesn't matter what the heart is made out of; just what it does. For example, conscious pains are defined more in terms of input and output, such as they are caused by bodily damage and cause avoidance behavior, as well as in terms of their relationship to other mental states.

MARY: Yeah, although functionalism doesn't necessarily entail materialism, it's still normally viewed as materialistic since virtually all functionalists also believe that something physical ultimately realizes that functional state in the organism.

DAVE: I guess one advantage though is that it can easily accommodate the multiple realizability of mental states that we discussed earlier as a problem for type-identity theory.

MARY: Yes, but one serious objection to functionalism is that any purely functional account of conscious mental states cannot adequately explain, or just entirely leaves out, the essentially subjective "feel" of conscious states. It may even be possible to have two functionally equivalent creatures where one of them lacks qualia entirely. This is the **absent qualia** objection. Having the right inputs and outputs aren't enough to have pains, color experiences, or taste sensations. The term **qualia** is most often understood as the felt properties or qualities of conscious states. It's just a fancy philosopher's term for the qualitative or phenomenal properties of mental states.

STEVE: So let's drop it here, because I really want to get into a different serious puzzle with materialism.

DAVE: Actually, I do too. What problem do you have in mind, Steve? Why don't you start? I may have one later.

2.5 The Knowledge Argument and Property Dualism

STEVE: OK. This is a problem about the inability of materialism to explain consciousness, that is, our subjective first-person experience. We can very generally call it the **materialist problem of consciousness** which is related to what Joseph Levine calls the **explanatory gap** between the physical and mental, that is, the inability of materialism to reduce consciousness to something in physical terms. A similar well-known worry raised by David Chalmers is called the **hard problem of consciousness**, that is, the difficulty of explaining just how physical processes in the brain give rise to specific subjective conscious experiences.

DAVE: Interesting, go on.

STEVE: We should first keep in mind that even though the term 'conscious' is notoriously ambiguous, the most commonly used notion of **conscious** among philosophers is captured by Thomas Nagel's famous "what it is like" sense. That is, when I'm in a conscious mental state, there is "something it is like" for me to be in that state from the subjective or first-person point of view. When I smell a flower or have a conscious visual perception, there is something it "seems like" from my perspective.

MARY: Sounds fine to me. I do think we must keep in mind that this is what we're trying to explain.

STEVE: So, I mainly have in mind the famous thought experiment from philosopher Frank Jackson, which is sometimes called the **knowledge argument**. He initially argued that it supported epiphenomenalism, but he no longer thinks so. Still, I think a significant problem for materialism remains. Let's suppose that we knew everything about the brain of a conscious lower animal, such as a cat or a bat. In other words, Mary, suppose that we did in fact have perfect knowledge about the cat brain.

MARY: Sounds great!

STEVE: We would therefore, according to materialism, have all of the third-person physical knowledge about the mind of a cat. Right?

MARY: Sure, because the cat's mind *is* its brain.

STEVE: OK, but wouldn't a materialist say that we would have all of the facts about the cat's mind, period?

MARY: I suppose so, because we would know everything about its brain.

STEVE: But this is where the problem comes in. It seems obvious to me that there would still be something about the cat's mind that we didn't know.

MARY: Like what?

STEVE: The way that cats experience the world, that is, what we might call 'what it is like to be a cat.' And the same would go for any other creature that is different from us. We would not understand certain subjective facts about the cat's 'point of view' on the world.

MARY: Maybe not, but why is this a problem for the materialist?

STEVE: Well, at least one way to understand materialism is to say that *all* of the facts about someone's mind are physical facts. So if we knew everything about a brain, then we would know everything about a mind. But clearly this would not happen. Even if we had all of the scientific knowledge about a cat's brain, there'd be many facts left out. These could only be 'mental facts,' which are not reducible to the physical. That is, some things can only be known from the *subjective perspective*. Therefore, materialism is inherently flawed when it comes to explaining consciousness and consciousness cannot be reduced to the physical.

DAVE: I like that, Steve. And the crucial consequence for physical science is that we could never come to know everything about the world through science. Even in an ideal future in which everything physical is known by us, something would still be left out of the story. Objective physical facts can be grasped from any point of view, but some facts are essentially limited to a subjective point of view. Steve's story reminds me of a similar argument.

MARY: Maybe, Dave, you should give your similar argument now. Then I can try to tackle both at once.

DAVE: OK. Suppose, Mary, that your older sister Maria had been radically color blind from birth so that she could only discern shades of white, gray, and black. Partly because of her condition and of hearing others talk about colors she can't see, she has become very interested in color perception.

MARY: Interesting, go on.

DAVE: Suppose that, as in Steve's story, she learns *everything* about color perception in humans. Science has also advanced so much that she really knows everything about what goes on in normal humans when we perceive red. So she has all of the neurophysiological information or knowledge about "having a red experience."

STEVE: I think I see where you are going.

MARY: Me too, so get there.

DAVE: Of course. Suppose further that a miraculous surgical technique becomes available that gives Maria normal color perception for the very first time. Now, immediately after the operation her eyes are covered with a bandage that is subsequently removed by the doctor. It again just seems obvious that Maria comes to learn or know something new when she first looks at a red wall, namely, what it's like to have a "reddish" color experience. And the same goes for any other color experience.

STEVE: Right. So we must ask: What did Maria learn upon seeing the red wall and upon having her first 'reddish experience'? Since she already had all of the physical information, Maria must have gained some nonphysical information or some unique mental fact that could only be acquired by actually having the experience. So not all information or knowledge about the mind is physical information, and therefore, materialism is false.

MARY: Very thought provoking examples, but I don't think they spell doom for materialism. I know of quite a few responses to them in the philosophical literature. Three come to mind. Let me briefly explain.

STEVE: Let's have number one.

MARY: *First*, in Maria's case, maybe, prior to the operation, she'd be able to imagine what various colors would look like given her omniscience about the neuropsychology of color. She might've been able to "conjure up" reddish images in her mind because of what she knew. Just as we can picture or imagine some objects without actually having experienced them, so Maria might have been able to do this with color experiences even before the surgery.

DAVE: Are you serious?

MARY: Sure. You must remember that, in your story, she knew *everything* about color perception. That's a lot! And we shouldn't underestimate what might follow from that fact. How can you be so sure that such a person wouldn't be able to imagine or visualize what certain colors would look like?

DAVE: I guess I can't be absolutely sure, but it hardly seems likely. When we normally conjure up imaginary visual images, we only combine in our minds previously seen objects or properties. But this is not so for Maria since she has never had any color experiences except for shades of black and white.

MARY: I don't see how you could rule it out. It's very difficult to understand completely now just how much knowledge we're talking about.

STEVE: Do you think something similar might be true about the cat story?

MARY: I'm not sure if it applies there. Of course if we knew everything about cat neurophysiology we'd be better able to imagine what it's like to be a cat, but because cat and human brains are so different and we just don't have cat brains, we'd probably still fall short.

STEVE: Doesn't that concern you?

MARY: Not really. It brings me to my *second* reply: How did you get from the total knowledge about the cat's brain to a denial of materialism? You seem to be confusing epistemology, or a knowledge related claim, with the more metaphysical identity claim made by materialism.

STEVE: How do you mean?

MARY: Even if we were omniscient about cat neurophysiology but didn't really know what it was like to be a cat, I don't see how this shows that the cat's mental states aren't just its brain states. Even Dave admitted last night that he believed materialism is probably correct for animals.

DAVE: Yes, but there remains the deeper problem of the explanatory limitations of materialism. Perhaps this is the primary lesson to be learned from Steve's cat story.

MARY: But materialism as a metaphysical claim about mind-brain identity seems unaffected. As a matter of fact, I think that our continuing puzzlement over cat experience should be expected. After all, only the cat is having the experiences and is actually undergoing its brain processes. Given that our brains are different from cat brains, it seems natural for there to be certain aspects of their experience that we could never fully comprehend. I suspect this would be so for many cross-species examples. Actually, that's often likely true within our species. I mean, do I know "what it is like" to throw the winning touchdown pass in the Super Bowl or break a gymnastics record in an Olympic event? Probably not in at least some sense. But I don't see how any of this refutes the central claim of materialism: mental states are neural or brain states.

Dave: But how does this apply to my story about Maria?

Mary: Similarly, it shouldn't come as a surprise if she didn't know 'what it is like to experience red' before the surgery. But that is because she was incapable, prior to the surgery, of undergoing the relevant brain processes despite all of her neurophysiological knowledge.

Dave: So then you admit that Maria does learn something new after the surgery? And, if so, wouldn't it have to be something nonphysical?

Mary: No, and I'm not even sure that she does learn anything new. There are crucial ambiguities in your questions that make it seem as if materialism has a problem here.

Dave: Like what? Does Maria learn something new or not?

Mary: This brings me to a *third* response, which is a bit more technical.

Dave: We'll try to follow.

Mary: You talk about learning some new *fact* or *piece of information* in Maria's story. In short, you think that she gains some further *knowledge* when she experiences red for the first time.

Dave: Yes.

Mary: But, first of all, we should distinguish between two types of knowledge: 'knowing that' or 'factual knowledge' which involves knowing that some fact or statement is true; and 'knowledge by acquaintance,' which involves a more experiential type of knowing. For example, again, I know that Babe Ruth hit sixty home runs in the 1927 season, but I have no personal experience by which I acquired such knowledge. So, in this case, I know a *fact*, but I do not have knowledge by acquaintance of that same fact.

STEVE: OK. I see the distinction, and I see how we could come up with many more examples. We often know that something is the case in the absence of direct knowledge by acquaintance.

MARY: Good. Well, Maria does *not* lack any factual knowledge about color perception. By your hypothesis she has it all! So she doesn't learn any new facts or information when she first experiences red.

DAVE: I'm not so sure about that. Doesn't she learn some new 'mental fact'?

MARY: I don't see why. If we found a videotape of Babe Ruth's sixtieth home run during 1927 and watched it, would we come to learn some new fact about his home run total in 1927?

STEVE: I suppose not. We would only experience that same fact or event in a new way.

MARY: Exactly, and this also goes for Maria. After the surgery, Maria does not come to learn a new fact but only comes to know *the same fact in a different way.* She had the factual knowledge and then comes to have knowledge by acquaintance of what it's like to have a reddish experience. But no new nonphysical "mental fact" is learned and so there's no reason for the materialist to be embarrassed here. There isn't any additional mental fact that eludes materialism, but only a different way to learn about that same fact through experience.

DAVE: Sounds strange to me. And I'm not sure about your 'Babe Ruth' analogy. It just seems so obvious that Maria would've gained some additional knowledge not included in her prior physical knowledge.

MARY: But think of it in terms of last night's discussion. Remember Leibniz's Law, co-referring terms, first- and third-person perspectives, and so on?

DAVE: Sure.

MARY: From the third-person perspective, Maria is omniscient with respect to the relevant physical and neural properties. But then, after the surgery, she becomes acquainted with the same neural property from the first-person perspective, that is, by undergoing the neural process herself. The neural property isn't new; only the perspective is. Surely this is no threat to materialism.

STEVE: How do co-referring terms or expressions fit in?

MARY: There will always be at least two different names or expressions referring to the brain process responsible for a color experience. One will be in the language of neurophysiology and the other in terms of a first-person description such as "the experience seems to me to be such-and-such." Before the surgery, Maria knew about the property only under the neurophysiological description. After the surgery, she comes to know about that same property under a first-person description. Some philosophers call these **phenomenal concepts**, that is, concepts that use a phenomenal or "first-person" property to refer to some conscious mental state. So why the big mystery?

STEVE: I'll need to think about it a bit more. And, actually, there's even a more radical skepticism called **mysterianism**, which is the view that we are simply not capable of solving the problem of consciousness. Mysterians, such as Colin McGinn, believe that the hard problem can *never* be solved because of human cognitive limitations and that the explanatory gap can't be closed. Our concept-forming mechanisms simply will not allow us to grasp the physical and causal basis of consciousness. We access consciousness through introspection or the first-person perspective, but our access to the brain is through the use of outer spatial senses, like vision, which is a more third-person perspective. So we have no way to access both the brain and consciousness *together* and any explanatory link between them is forever beyond our reach.

MARY: Wow; that is rather radical.

DAVE: Maybe not.

STEVE: Well, that's even too skeptical for me. I'm not quite sure how we can rule out a solution forever. That seems extremely pessimistic. We might wonder, for example, why we can't combine the two perspectives within certain experimental contexts.

MARY: And, you know, maybe the hard problem isn't really so hard after all—it'll just take some more time. After all, the sciences of chemistry and biology didn't develop overnight and we are probably relatively early in the history of neurophysiology and consciousness studies. Maybe the hard problem is more like the old "vitalism" problem of how "life" emerges from "matter." No real mystery there anymore given all the advances in biology and genetics. So how can success for a reductionistic strategy on consciousness be ruled out so soon? It seems premature to declare that any kind of successful physicalist reduction is hopeless.

DAVE: Maybe, but I still think there's something which materialism must always leave out in any *explanation* of conscious experience. I just don't see how the mind or consciousness could be *reduced* to materialistic explanations even if substance dualism is incorrect. This is probably why so-called **property dualism** is more popular with philosophers these days. It says that there are mental *properties* (that is, characteristics or aspects of things), as opposed to substances, that are neither identical with, nor reducible to, physical properties. There are different versions of property dualism, but what they have in common is the idea that conscious properties, such as the color qualia involved in a conscious visual perception, cannot be explained in purely physical terms. The sharpness of pain, for example, is surely not a property of a brain state. Any genuine claim of **reductionism** should involve a relation between theories such that one theory (the reduced theory) is derivable from another theory (the reducing theory) usually with the help of "bridging principles." But I just don't see how materialism can succeed in doing so.

STEVE: But I'm not even sure I understand what it means to say that a 'property' is mental, or 'nonphysical' in some sense, without inhering in at least some kind of substance? Does it even make sense to say that some instances of nonphysical properties occur in one's physical body?

MARY: And even if materialism does have a real problem here, dualism is much worse off. Dave, you can't tell me that dualism can explain consciousness any better. Indeed, it would again seem impossible for dualism to explain it for some of the reasons we discussed last night. It would be like giving up! At least we're trying to explain consciousness.

STEVE: I agree with you on that, Mary.

DAVE: Maybe. But you, Mary, are the one who claims that you'll be able to explain consciousness someday. So isn't it fair to ask where such a scientific investigation might lead and whether any problems would permanently persist?

MARY: Sure, but I think there are good replies to both of your examples.

STEVE: Perhaps. But maybe this difficulty with the reduction of the mental to physical is why some are still even tempted to opt for **panpsychism**, which is the view that all things in physical reality, even down to micro-particles, have some degree of mentality or consciousness. If consciousness didn't arise or emerge at some point from "dead matter" or during the evolution of life, then perhaps it always existed in some form from the start.

DAVE: But there just seems to be such a lack of evidence that fundamental entities possess minds, let alone some level of consciousness. Atoms and photons, not to mention tables, rocks, and beer bottles, lack the characteristic evidence of consciousness, such as complex behavior, the ability to learn, and so on.

STEVE: I have to say that I'm a bit puzzled by the recent resurgent interest in panpsychism.

MARY: Me too. And another objection to panpsychism is the so-called combination problem: If mind or consciousness is supposed to exist in quarks, atoms, photons, or cells, then human minds must be some kind of combination or sum of these lesser minds. But how do the experiences of fundamental entities combine to produce the familiar human conscious experience that we have? It is very difficult to see how this question could be answered. Further, if a panpsychist is motivated to reject materialism due to its inability to explain the connection between the brain and consciousness, doesn't a similar problem simply reappear at the micro-level?

STEVE: I see.

MARY: And, again, I don't want to make it sound like materialists already have all the answers. For example, there is what's called the **binding problem**.

DAVE: What's that?

MARY: It's the problem of how the brain *integrates* information processed by different regions of the brain, such as the color, motion, and shape of a thrown ball. It's still unclear just how the brain allows us to experience what's sometimes called the **unity of consciousness**. There are many different senses of "unity," but perhaps most common is the notion that, from the first-person point of view, we experience the world in an integrated way and as a single phenomenal field of experience. However, when one looks at how the brain processes information, one only sees discrete regions of the cortex processing separate aspects of perceptual objects. There's really no central place in the brain where all this information comes together.

DAVE: Sounds like the materialist version of the combination problem.

MARY: Fair enough. There are also further extreme cases of "disunity," such as dissociative identity disorder, but again, I don't see how dualism helps.

STEVE: Me either. Well, I have to go. Let's talk again tomorrow. I do want to discuss something else.

DAVE: Same time, same place!

THE THIRD NIGHT

3.1 The Problem of Other Minds

MARY: What do you want to discuss tonight?

DAVE: Steve had something in mind.

STEVE: Yeah. Some of our conversation last night took on an epistemological tone, that is, it dealt with issues of knowledge. I would like to discuss the **problem of other minds** which is perhaps the most traditional epistemological problem in philosophy of mind.

DAVE: Good idea. Can you describe the basic problem as you see it?

STEVE: Actually, we could divide it into two subproblems or subquestions: (1) How can I know that another creature or thing has a conscious mind at all? and (2) How could I know whether another creature or thing has the same particular experiences or mental states that I do?

MARY: Right. It seems important to distinguish between these questions because I may be reasonably sure that you *have a mind*, but more skeptical about whether or not you experience the world in the same way that I do. In other words, answering question (1) will often be easier than answering (2). We saw this last night when we talked about cats. We assumed that cats have conscious minds but that needs to be independently supported. And the harder problem has to do with what precisely their conscious experiences are like.

DAVE: Right, but in neither case will such knowledge be as *certain* as the knowledge we have of our own minds. My knowledge that I have a conscious mind is about as certain as it gets. It's even one of Descartes' indubitable truths. Of course, very few truths have such a lofty status and very little knowledge is so absolutely certain.

MARY: Sure, and the problem is not limited to other *human* minds. We should also discuss various animal minds and the possibility of conscious machines or robots. Our ability to answer questions (1) and (2) will no doubt depend greatly on which type of thing we are asking about. I do have some doubts about whether certain very primitive creatures are conscious at all.

STEVE: I have serious doubts about the possibility of machine consciousness.

DAVE: Me too.

STEVE: But we often act as if we do know about other minds. For example, I think I know that both of you have minds, especially after the last two nights. If I know this, how do I know it?

MARY: Well, Dave is probably right that this cannot quite be absolutely certain knowledge. But it can be strong inductive knowledge based on good inductive reasoning. After all, most scientific knowledge is inductive and yet is not considered to be weakly grounded. For example, "all crows are black" and "the sun will rise tomorrow" are standard examples of inductive knowledge based on past observation and evidence.

DAVE: Right. Good inductive reasoning will take evidence and show how it strongly supports the truth of a conclusion, even if it doesn't absolutely guarantee it. At the least, the evidence should show that the conclusion is *probably* or *very likely* to be true. The nature of the evidence will depend on what the inquiry is.

STEVE: Of course. If knowledge had to be "absolutely certain," then I'm afraid that we would not know very much: perhaps only some truths about our own minds, mathematical truths, and some logical principles. In any case, we should at least strive for *rational belief* even if it falls short of knowledge, and we should always try to believe as rationally as possible. However, I still do have doubts about how well we can answer the two subquestions.

MARY: I sometimes do too, but I also think that dualism has a more serious problem here.

DAVE: Why?

MARY: Well, according to dualism, another human mind could never be observed. But materialists believe that we do observe other minds, or at least it's possible to do so. So answering the problem is more difficult for you.

DAVE: Must you assume materialism here too?

MARY: I'm not assuming it. I'm just pointing out how much more difficult it is to acquire knowledge of other minds if dualism is true.

DAVE: But that's only if you assume that the brain is part of the evidence for the existence of another mind.

MARY: Of course! It seems to me that it would be very strong evidence for answering question (1). That is, if someone has a human or humanlike brain, then it seems reasonable to believe that there's a conscious mind. Or at least it's very strong evidence for that conclusion. Don't you think so?

DAVE: I suppose so, but of course I don't believe that the mind just *is* the observed brain.

MARY: We know.

DAVE: Anyway, don't you think you know now that I have a mind?

MARY: Sure.

DAVE: But if you do know it, your current knowledge can't be based on any observation of my brain. You've never actually seen it.

MARY: No, but it seems reasonable to assume that it's in your skull because you appear from the outside to be a human being. It's no different from my clearly rational belief that you have lungs or a heart. And, again, it's at least possible for me to observe your mind or brain via X-ray, CAT scan, or brain surgery. But on your view we could never observe another human mind.

DAVE: Granted, but you must admit that as a matter of fact we don't typically use brain observation as evidence for the existence of another's mind.

MARY: Of course.

3.2 Evidence for Other Minds and Animal Consciousness

STEVE: Well, but in addition to brain structure, what other kinds of evidence can help us deal with this problem?

MARY: Another would be behavioral reactions to stimuli or bodily movements. For example, the fact that you try to avoid bodily damage normally indicates that you expect to feel something. If I kick you in the leg, you'll behave in a way that indicates the presence of consciousness. And, for that matter, the same goes for many animals, such as dogs and cats. This would be some evidence that another creature has the capacity to feel pain. Last night we agreed that mental events cause bodily movements. So when we observe behavioral effects it's reasonable to infer the existence of some mental cause. I know that this is what happens in my case and it's reasonable to assume the same is true when I observe others behaving in similar ways.

DAVE: Right. Another piece of evidence has to do with the ability to use language or to communicate. We've communicated over the past two nights by using the English language. This seems to be good evidence that you have a conscious mind and in particular that you have conscious thoughts, which you express through language. Even whales are able to communicate in their own way. Although they can't communicate *with us*, it's pretty obvious they can do so with each other. The same goes for many other animal species.

MARY: There are also three other related kinds of evidence, which can help answer the problem of other minds.

STEVE: What are they?

MARY: They have to do with the ability to learn, the ability to solve problems, and creativity. For example, your ability to learn from a teacher provides some evidence that you have a conscious mind. It seems to require some conscious memory and thought. Furthermore, you're able to solve problems in your everyday life. Even many lower animals when confronted with a challenging or unexpected situation are able to "figure out" what to do. This ability seems to require having a conscious thought process. As did early homo sapiens, many lower animals have figured out ways to find food or to hunt, such as by making tools and weapons. And solving problems often involves a certain degree of creativity, which requires conscious thinking; for example, the human ability to build bridges or to write philosophical articles. Creating artworks generally seems to indicate consciousness, reasoning, and planning.

DAVE: So let's agree on these four types of evidence which can help us to answer our original questions. Let's call them "the four conditions" and number them as follows (*he writes them down on a piece of paper*):

(1) Brain Structure
(2) Nonverbal or Nonvocal Behavioral Evidence
(3) Ability to Use Language and/or to Communicate
(4) Ability to Learn, Ability to Solve Problems, and/or Creativity

STEVE: OK. You're both right that they're probably what we implicitly use when making judgments about whether or not another creature has a mind. But none of them *individually* can conclusively prove that another has a conscious mind.

MARY: You're probably right about that, but can you elaborate?

STEVE: Well, let's just look at the first subquestion: How can I know that another creature or thing has a conscious mind at all? Of course, we must remember that our confidence in answering it will greatly depend on which "creature" or "thing" we're examining. So we really have many different questions. But if we take each of the four conditions individually, we'll find that none of them can establish knowledge that another creature has a mind.

DAVE: In other words, can you think of cases where the evidence for meeting one condition is present but where we might still remain very skeptical about the existence of a conscious mind?

STEVE: Yes. Let's take each one. If another human has a brain structure similar to ours, how can we be sure that he's conscious? Suppose I show you a brain X-ray which resembles a typical human brain. You can't be sure that a conscious mind is associated with that brain.

MARY: Why not?

STEVE: It could be the brain of a coma patient or even of a recently deceased person. So there would be no consciousness.

DAVE: I'm sure that we can respond to that one, but let's first hear about the other three conditions.

STEVE: Sure. The second condition might also fall short by itself. Ants, flies, and insects display "avoidance behavior" when we try to kill them in our apartments, but I doubt that most of them are *consciously* thinking or feeling fear. We may also someday be able to build a robot that can behaviorally react in familiar ways. But I doubt if that would suffice to prove that robots have conscious minds. So appropriate behavioral reactions to stimuli cannot, by themselves, show that something has a conscious mind. Even a single-celled amoeba moves away from certain harmful fluids, but it seems unlikely that a single cell is conscious.

MARY: What about the last two conditions?

STEVE: Well, cognitive scientists and engineers often speak of computers as having a language and as communicating things to us. But I don't think that we should conclude that current computers are conscious. Also, you know that bees, for example, communicate to each other where honey can be found through a series of rather complicated "dances."

MARY: Yes, it's a fascinating phenomenon and amazing to watch.

STEVE: But I'm not quite convinced, on that basis alone, that they're consciously relaying any such complicated thoughts.

MARY: Maybe, but go on.

STEVE: You talked about creativity. Perhaps it *often* indicates the presence of consciousness, but what about the way that spiders make their webs? It's an incredible phenomenon and one that seems to involve creativity in the way that they make different and very complex webs at different times. But I'm not quite sure that spiders are conscious creatures at all.

MARY: Fine, but I'm not sure that deserves to be called "creative."

STEVE: And the ability to learn or to solve problems is clearly not sufficient for consciousness. We can program computers to solve chess or mathematical problems, but no one believes that this is good evidence of a conscious mind. Actually, most computers can solve some of these problems better than humans. Also, rats and mice can "learn" many things through conditioning. But I suppose one might at least still wonder if they're conscious or that they're consciously remembering or thinking during the conditioning process.

DAVE: I don't agree with all of your claims, but even if we grant them for the sake of argument, you have obviously only shown that none of the four conditions *individually* can *conclusively prove* that another creature has a conscious mind.

STEVE: Sure, but why exactly is that so important?

DAVE: Two reasons: First, we've already agreed that knowledge of other minds would at most be strongly inductive, that is, it would only establish a likelihood that another has a conscious mind. "Absolute certainty" or "conclusive proof" isn't the issue and is rarely achieved. *Strong evidence for a reasonable belief* is the issue. Remember?

STEVE: Fair enough.

DAVE: Second, even if you're right that no single condition is, by itself, strong enough evidence to support the conclusion that another has a mind, more than one condition would be, and the more conditions met, the more likely that the creature in question has a conscious mind.

MARY: Right! I like to think of it as a prosecutor trying to build a case against a defendant. There will rarely, if ever, be one single piece of evidence which conclusively proves his guilt beyond a reasonable doubt. Perhaps a confession by the accused or convincing testimony by an eyewitness, but the confession could have been coerced or the eyewitness could simply have mistaken a similar looking person for the defendant.

STEVE: Sure. Even apparently damning evidence such as a fingerprint at the scene of the crime or possession of the murder weapon could involve an innocent person.

DAVE: Yeah, maybe the fingerprint was left on an earlier occasion and the murder weapon was planted by the real killer.

MARY: Anyway, my point is that many different pieces of evidence are required which when taken together strongly indicate the guilt of the defendant beyond a reasonable doubt, even if not beyond any doubt whatsoever. But in order to win the case the prosecutor typically also needs to show, for example, some evidence of motive and opportunity, and some other evidence tying the defendant to the scene. In such cases, we justifiably say that we know the defendant is guilty. Similarly, in trying to determine whether another creature or object has a conscious mind, we must look at the whole range of evidence and the degree to which each type can be established.

STEVE: That seems right, but let's get down to specific examples.

MARY: Sure, let's start with human minds. How do I know that you or any other human has a conscious mind? You meet all four conditions. You presumably have a brain much like mine and this can be observed. Moreover, you display various behavioral reactions to stimuli, such as avoiding tripping over chairs and driving through green lights only. You also satisfy conditions three and four: you are able to use language to communicate and you demonstrate by your philosophical comments and arguments your creativity and prob-lem-solving ability. So I think I know that you and, by extension, any other human being has a conscious mind.

DAVE: And this would explain how your first counterexample could be answered.

STEVE: The one about the coma patient or the dead person?

DAVE: Yes. The reason we couldn't know that the coma patient or a dead person has a conscious mind has to do with conditions two, three, and four. These three conditions wouldn't obviously be satis-fied. Actually, it isn't even clear to me that even the first condition is satisfied since we probably should take it to mean a properly *func-tioning* brain, not merely the brain structure itself.

STEVE: Of course, but small infants are not creative and can't use lan-guage. Severely retarded humans also have difficulty meeting con-ditions three and four.

MARY: Right, but they satisfy conditions one and two and really can communicate to some extent. So don't you think they meet enough conditions to warrant a claim of knowledge?

STEVE: Sure, but you see how it can get complicated almost immediately.

MARY: Yes. I never said it would always be easy, but applying the four conditions does seem to be a useful strategy for dealing with the problem of other minds.

DAVE: Let me also add a point here about their usefulness. At the other extreme, we might ask how we know that, say, rocks and plants aren't conscious. The answer is that they don't meet any of the four conditions. That is, a rock doesn't have a brain or anything like a nervous system. Nor does it behaviorally react in the way that conscious creatures do when kicked or stepped on. Neither do rocks try to avoid potentially "painful" experiences. The same goes for plants and trees: they don't jump out of the way when we cut them or scream when a saw gets near them. There's also no reason to believe that rocks or plants use language or communicate to us or to one another. Finally, rocks and plants don't learn anything and display no ability to solve problems.

STEVE: Sure, but the real hard questions have to do with the "in-between" cases. Perhaps we clearly know that other humans are conscious and that plants and rocks are not, but what about the unclear cases where only some of the conditions are met? And what about when the evidence conflicts?

MARY: Such as?

STEVE: Let's go back to my earlier examples. The behavior of certain flies and insects may suggest consciousness, but I seriously doubt that most of them are conscious creatures.

MARY: Well, this is a case where the creature probably doesn't satisfy the other three conditions. Flies and worms, for example, do not have anything like a true brain with extensive neurons and a nervous system. They also clearly fail to meet conditions three and four. So we might agree that flies are not conscious because they fail to meet most of the conditions. At least we would have an explanation. Some primitive creatures, such as moths, may have evolved in a purely nonconscious way. If we go by the evidence, we should seriously doubt that they are conscious.

DAVE: And your single-celled organism example can be explained in a similar way. It should be obvious that amoebas can't satisfy conditions one, three, and four.

STEVE: Fine, but are you saying you know that such organisms are not conscious?

DAVE: In some cases, yes. For example, the evidence is overwhelming against rocks and plants, so it's reasonable to claim that we know they lack consciousness. I think we can say the same about single-celled organisms and some insects. At the least, we can justifiably assert that it's highly unlikely. That is, it's reasonable to believe that they do not have conscious minds.

STEVE: How about my bee example?

MARY: That's a bit tougher because bees seem to satisfy two of the four conditions. Like flies and insects, they meet condition two, and in addition they do have that rather sophisticated ability to communicate that was mentioned earlier. So condition three seems satisfied to some extent, but I'm not sure about conditions one and four.

STEVE: I agree, so what's your solution here?

MARY: I confess that I'm not sure about whether we can know, at least right now, that bees and some other insects have conscious minds. That is, whether we could know either way. But one possibility is that, when the evidence is divided, we should ask whether one condition should carry more weight than the others. This way we can better form a reasonable opinion. I am inclined to use similar enough brain structure as the tiebreaker, but I want to come back to this in a little while.

DAVE: Much the same goes for spiders. They clearly meet condition two, but I doubt if they meet conditions one and three.

MARY: Right, spiders are probably in that gray area with bees.

DAVE: Yes, but I sometimes wonder if a spider's ability to make webs really deserves to be called "creative." Such behavior may just be purely nonconscious innate activity that does not require any conscious thinking or planning at all. So perhaps we should conclude that spiders are not conscious since they really only satisfy the second condition.

STEVE: How would the four conditions apply to other animals?

DAVE: Apes and gorillas, for example, would clearly satisfy all four conditions. Their brains are similar enough to ours, although they do not have as much cerebral cortex, the brain area responsible for our more sophisticated mental abilities. They often react as we do to external stimuli. They also at least have some ability to communicate with us and especially with one another, to use primitive languages, and to solve certain limited problems.

MARY: Right, and we're not saying that they satisfy conditions three and four *to the same degree* as humans. But the overall evidence seems sufficient to establish that they're conscious creatures.

STEVE: I suppose so. I guess the same would go for animals such as lions, bears, pigs, tigers, cats, dogs, and so on.

MARY: I think so, even though the evidence will perhaps be somewhat weaker. For example, a cat brain is not nearly as sophisticated as an ape brain. Also, cats surely do not have the same communication or learning abilities as higher mammals. But I don't think that this should cause us to doubt that they have conscious minds.

DAVE: And dogs, for example, can be trained to do some rather amazing things which go well beyond mere "conditioning." Just think about the mental abilities required for being a seeing-eye or police dog, not to mention their superior sense of smell. It would be very odd to suppose that they are unconscious creatures. Why would a blind person want to have an unconscious dog?

STEVE: (*Steve laughs*) Fair enough, but aside from insects, are there any other animals or creatures which you really doubt are conscious at all? That is, which animals do you think are not likely to be conscious?

DAVE: Sometimes I do wonder about mice, rats, and even frogs for some of the reasons mentioned concerning bees and spiders. But I'd bet that they are capable of having at least some primitive conscious mental states, such as pain and perceptions.

MARY: I wonder, for example, about snakes and lobster. However, I do know that even they have more advanced brains than is sometimes believed. So I tend to give them the benefit of the doubt.

STEVE: So then you do admit that it's difficult to answer the first subquestion regarding many lower animals or creatures.

MARY: Sure. I don't want to give the impression that I have all the answers, even using the four conditions as our basis. But I do think that it's a good strategy for dealing with the problem of other minds.

STEVE: But of course you must admit that the problem only gets more difficult when we try to answer the second subquestion: How could I know that another creature or thing has the same particular experiences or mental states that I do? Even if we can know that a cat has a conscious mind, we saw last night that it seems much more difficult to know precisely what a cat's conscious experience is like at a particular time. And the same would go for many of the other animals we've discussed tonight.

DAVE: I agree with that.

STEVE: Right. How do we know what a dog feels when we step on its paw? How do we know what a lion is thinking or feeling while it's chasing a deer? How do we know what it's like for an eagle to soar over the cliffs? How could I know what kind of visual experience my dog is having as it sits next to me on my porch? And so on and so on. We surely can't assume that they experience things in the same way that we do.

MARY: Maybe not, but perhaps we can look to the four conditions for *some* help. For example, a dog's reaction when we step on its paw seems to indicate that it feels something very unpleasant, probably much as we do when someone steps on our bare foot. Plus, dogs do share with us some lower brain structure.

STEVE: But conditions three and four are useless here. For example, no animal can ever really tell us what its experience is like. We simply interpret its behavior as best we can.

DAVE: And even the first condition might often be unhelpful. It can help *rule out* the possibility that a creature has a certain type of conscious state because it simply lacks the relevant brain structure. But merely knowing that an animal has a visual cortex of a certain kind can't tell us everything about its specific moment-to-moment visual experiences.

MARY: I agree that this is a more difficult problem but I'm trying to be a bit more optimistic, especially to the extent that the neurosciences can help.

STEVE: We do of course have to be careful not to anthropomorphize, on the one hand, but it's also important not to underestimate animal minds, on the other hand. Still, it's clear that we've come a long way from Descartes' view that animals are mere "automata" and that animals do not even have conscious experience. Perhaps his view was at least partly based on the fact that he was a substance dualist, didn't know much about our comparative brains, and that he thought only humans have a "soul" and an afterlife.

DAVE: I suppose that's possible. I can understand the issue there.

MARY: There's also the practical matter of the morality of animal experimentation and eating animals. At the very least, whether or not an animal can suffer and feel pain should be taken into account with regard to how they ought to be treated. Billions of animals are killed every year for food and research, and many of them are subjected to rather cruel conditions.

STEVE: Yeah, that's important to keep in mind.

MARY: I wanted to get back to animal brains though. I took the seminar on animal consciousness last semester, which was excellent. From what I recall, many animals, including some non-mammals, do at least share with us some of the more basic areas of our brain, such as the amygdala in the limbic system and various sensory cortices, responsible for emotions and perceptions, respectively. On the other hand, to the extent that animals lack some of our brain structures which are responsible for more sophisticated mental capacities, such as the prefrontal cortex, it seems reasonable to suppose that they are not capable of having these kinds of mental states.

STEVE: Which mental capacities?

MARY: Well, for example, an ability to plan, reason, and reflect on one's own mental states.

STEVE: I can see that. Plus, this is also where behavioral evidence can corroborate. Hey, there aren't any cat or lizard philosophy clubs as far as I know (*Steve laughs*).

DAVE: I was also in that seminar. I recall reading about how crabs react to analgesics in the same way that honeybees do. If crabs feel pain, then surely bees also do since bees have ten times more neurons than crabs.

MARY: Actually, I think that bee brain *density* is ten times greater than a mammalian cerebral cortex. Also, I learned that the fish consciousness literature has exploded.

STEVE: Really?

MARY: Yeah, trout, for example, also respond well to painkillers when exposed to noxious stimuli and fish generally react to morphine much as we do. We also discussed some interesting behavioral indicators of consciousness, such as "trade-off" behavior where, for example, fish decrease feeding attempts when electric shocks are increased but only until food deprivation increases. There is also something called "navigational detouring" which requires an animal to pursue a series of non-rewarding intermediate goals in order to obtain a greater ultimate reward. It does indeed often seem difficult to explain these sorts of behaviors entirely without also attributing consciousness, such as pain, pleasure, and fear.

STEVE: Now that is very interesting. I should look at the literature more closely.

MARY: My favorite observations from that class had to do with animal memory and so-called **mindreading**, which seem to be fairly sophisticated abilities indicating consciousness.

STEVE: What about memory?

MARY: Well, for example, scrub jays are food-caching birds, and when they have food they can't eat, they hide it and recover it later. Because some of the food is preferred but perishable, such as crickets, it must be eaten within a few days. Other food, such as nuts, is less preferred but doesn't perish as quickly. Scrub jays are shown, even days after caching, to know not only *what* kind of food was *where* but also *when* they had cached it. Although still somewhat controversial, these experimental results at least seem to show that scrub jays have some episodic memory which involves a sense of self over time.

STEVE: Interesting. And what's "mindreading"?

DAVE: It's being able to have mental states and mental concepts directed at someone else's mind. You know, for example, I know that you can hear the bell ring or that you believe that I'm in pain.

STEVE: That does seem fairly sophisticated.

MARY: Right, so it turns out that many crows and scrub jays return alone to caches they had hidden in the presence of others and re-cache them in new places. This suggests that they know that *others* know or see where the food is cached, and thus, to avoid having their food stolen, they re-cache the food.

STEVE: Wow. Now that's pretty amazing.

DAVE: We also read something about how rhesus monkeys attribute visual and auditory perceptions to others in competitive situations. For example, rhesus monkeys attempt to obtain food silently only in those conditions where silence was relevant to obtaining the food undetected. While a human competitor was looking away, monkeys would take grapes from a silent container, thus apparently understanding that their human competitors would hear the noise otherwise. Subjects reliably picked the container that did not alert the experimenter that a grape was being removed.

MARY: The same might go for any evidence of empathy and deception in some species which would seem to show that an animal can think about another's suffering and that an animal can cause another to have a false belief.

STEVE: So I guess much of this would fall under condition two, that is, nonverbal or nonvocal behavioral evidence for animal consciousness. I can see how these more sophisticated experiments might really help the case for attributing consciousness to various animals.

MARY: Yeah, that sounds right.

3.3 Alien Minds?

STEVE: Very interesting. Could we shift gears and discuss the other minds problem in a very different way?

DAVE: Sure.

STEVE: Let's talk about aliens. Suppose a UFO landed on earth and three little things emerged. How would we know whether they are purely unconscious sophisticated robots sent by intelligent life on another planet or whether they are conscious creatures? I don't think that the answer would be easy.

MARY: Why not? Let's say that we were able to capture them and observe them for a long period of time in a large scientific lab. No doubt everyone would be interested in observing them: philosophers, psychologists, neuroscientists. Why wouldn't we be able to gather enough information to make a reasonable judgment?

STEVE: Well, maybe we could in some cases, but look at the four conditions we've been using. Looking inside their "heads" at "brain structure" would probably be useless.

MARY: Why? It might show that there really is no "brain" at all, but rather something more mechanical or machinelike.

STEVE: Maybe, but how could we tell whether that 'something' could sustain consciousness?

MARY: Well, this is a difficult separate question which we can discuss later. But let's assume for now that the creature has something complex enough to be called a brain as we typically use the word. It seems that we'd then be fairly sure that the alien is conscious.

STEVE: But what basis could we have for judging that the "brain structure" of the alien provides evidence of consciousness? We all agreed last night that alien brains would probably be radically different from ours. After all, aliens would be from a very different environment and probably composed of radically different kinds of matter. This was part of your reason for not embracing type-materialism. Remember?

MARY: Yes, but it still seems possible to determine if a creature even with a very different brain is conscious.

STEVE: I don't see how. We'd have nothing to compare it to in order make such a judgment. We can't tell just by watching a complicated thing function. It's not as if the conscious states are revealed through our observation. Even in our own case, we only know that other humans and animals are conscious because we have a similar brain. But in the alien case no such comparison can be made. How could we know whether the creature was not merely some very intelligent complex machine?

DAVE: Good question. I have to agree with Steve's skepticism here. I don't think it would be so easy to tell even after extensive observation. And materialism won't help much either.

STEVE: Right, because you can't just observe or see that the alien has a conscious mind even if you believe that all mental processes are physical processes. We're trying to figure out whether the alien has a conscious mind in the first place.

MARY: Maybe we wouldn't know just by looking at the inside of its "head," but what about the other evidence?

STEVE: I think we run into similar problems with the other three conditions. It wouldn't be like *Star Trek* where most of the aliens look and behave very much like us, and where we can at least hear many of them speaking in English! Conditions two and three might almost be useless. We would likely have no way of communicating with them. Nor could we easily interpret their bodily reactions. How could we possibly know what is their "typical" or "normal" reaction to certain stimuli? And even if we could know, why would we expect it to be anything like ours?

MARY: Good questions, but over time we might be able to determine the way they normally react to certain stimuli and go from there. For example, they may not do what we normally do in the presence of intense heat but we can observe what they do over a long period of time.

STEVE: And then what? If they do nothing, we can't conclude that it's because they are not conscious, because heat might not affect them in the way it affects us. Maybe they come from a much hotter planet. And if they do react in a rather predictable way, it may only be a built-in nonconscious reaction, for example, like that of a sophisticated robot merely programmed to avoid a dangerous heat source.

MARY: Maybe, but then we should go on to see how they react to very cold temperatures. Perhaps this would cause them to react differently if they are from a hot planet. I mean, the evidence would take time to build up and analyze, but I think we could eventually form a reasonable conclusion. Some evidence might help to rule out consciousness and other evidence would support it. Also, you ignored condition four. Wouldn't we be able to determine whether the alien had learning or creative abilities through various testing techniques?

STEVE: Perhaps, but this wouldn't show that it is *consciously* learning or doing anything. Maybe it's a purely nonconscious robot with excellent learning abilities and built-in intelligence. We haven't been able to make such a robot yet but extraterrestrial beings may have been.

DAVE: Sounds right to me. And even if we became confident enough to answer subquestion one in a positive way, do you both see how much more difficult it is to answer the second subquestion?

STEVE: Of course. I mean, even if we were fairly sure that the alien had a conscious mind, it would be much more difficult to know how it experiences the world at any given moment. For example, what colors does it see?

MARY: Sure, that would be a problem, especially since their brains would not be similar to ours in many ways.

DAVE: Right.

3.4 Machine and Robot Consciousness

STEVE: Now what about machines or robots? They really do present some very interesting problems. Could a machine think or be conscious? Could a robot really subjectively experience smelling a rose or feeling pain? Is being alive, or a biological system, necessary for consciousness? If we built conscious robots, how should we treat them? Could robots have free will?

MARY: Yeah, this has fascinated popular culture and science fiction writers for a long time, such as in Isaac Asimov's *I, Robot* and the movie version that came out in 2004. Among television science fiction shows, probably my favorite robot character is Commander Data from *Star Trek: The Next Generation*. More recently, the TV series *Humans* explores many of those questions in a very vivid, interesting, and even somewhat disturbing way.

STEVE: Well, you know that there is a philosophical position which used to be called "machine functionalism." Much like we saw with functionalism last night, the idea at least seemed superior to other theories by allowing for multiple realizability, that is, the idea that the same kinds of mental states can be realized in different physical structures. But part of the overall attraction was the notion that, by analogy, the mind is to the brain as a computer program is to the hardware. I don't think this view is quite as prominent today.

MARY: Right, but in the background of the philosophical discussion is what has been called the "computational theory of mind" which says that the mind is basically a computational system and an information processor. The brain is thus thought of as a kind of digital computer where the main characteristic of computational theory is the manipulation of symbols.

DAVE: One of the obstacles has been programming a system to focus only on *relevant* information when attempting to solve a problem, which is a version of the so-called **frame problem**. Otherwise, too much time is spent solving the problem or performing a task and the system is not practically intelligent. Humans are surprisingly good at being able to zero in relatively quickly on what is relevant to a given task or problem. Further, we are also very good at recognizing what common sense and background knowledge is assumed in various contexts.

STEVE: In terms of the early literature, one very important paper— published in 1950—was written by the mathematician Alan Turing who proposed what has come to be known as the **Turing test** for machine intelligence and thought. The basic idea is that if a machine, hidden from view, could fool an interrogator into thinking that it was human, then we should say it thinks or, at least, has intelligence.

MARY: Yeah, Turing called it the "imitation game": Suppose that we have a person, a machine, and an interrogator. The interrogator is in a room separated from the other person and the machine. The object of the game is for the interrogator to determine which of the others is the person and which is the machine. The purpose of the machine is to try to cause the interrogator to mistakenly conclude that the machine is the person. The purpose of the person is to try to help the interrogator to correctly identify the machine.

DAVE: Part of the problem of course depends on whether or not one believes that thinking entails consciousness in some way and how one defines 'thinking.' Even if some robots now or in the future could pass the Turing test—a really big "if"—it isn't clear to me that it would be capable of thought, let alone consciousness. Turing was himself overly optimistic in his prediction. Still, some major advances have been made over the years.

STEVE: Sure, going back to chess playing machines including the IBM's impressive Deep Blue which defeated chess champion Gary Kasparov in 1997. There are also very useful programs to aid in medical diagnosis which work by narrowing down causes via an input of symptoms. But obviously one cannot ask these machines about virtually anything, as Turing had envisioned.

DAVE: Perhaps most impressive in recent years has been WATSON, which beat top champions on the game show *Jeopardy*. This is a major programming achievement both for breadth of knowledge and, perhaps even more importantly, the speed of access to relevant information. Again, if a machine or robot can't act in a timely way, then it's rather useless in many contexts. If we want robots to help the elderly with chores around the house, but it takes hours for the robots to bring medicine or water, this won't do.

MARY: But it occurs to me that you have both assumed that no "machine" or "robot" could be conscious while we were discussing alien minds. I'm not sure that we should rule out robot conscious-ness even if we can't build one now. Why are you?

STEVE: One reason is that they don't have organic brains at all. That is, they aren't composed of the kind of matter necessary for con-scious experience. I don't see how things made out of computer chips, metal, and wires could be conscious.

MARY: But you and Dave have also said that you don't understand how electrochemical reactions inside our skulls could achieve the same result. And maybe consciousness can be realized in all kinds of radically different substances.

STEVE: I just don't see how substances like metal and computer pro-grams could underlie consciousness or genuine "thinking." There just seems to be something very different about them. Maybe only organisms, as opposed to artifacts, can be conscious.

DAVE: How do you distinguish them?

STEVE: Well, organisms are biological individuals in an enduring spe-cies; they take in food and excrete wastes; they are nonrigid phys-ical objects; they reproduce through sexual intercourse; and so on. Artifacts, on the other hand, are built by organisms and made up of nonorganic material.

DAVE: I see. Interesting, Steve, maybe you're right about that.

MARY: Interesting how you, Dave, suddenly rely on all these biologi-cal facts. I thought you'd say that robots wouldn't have nonphysical minds or souls. I might agree at least that we're reluctant to attribute consciousness to machines because they aren't biological organisms, but it would also rule out God as conscious if you take it literally. See why?

DAVE: Well, yes, but I don't want to get into that. Why can't you allow for a unique exception and still appreciate the distinction?

MARY: I do appreciate the point, but you may fail to appreciate its consequences for theism, not to mention substance dualism. Any-way, I really do agree that this may be a natural factor in at least initially judging whether something has a conscious mind. But I'm just not sure how we can forever rule out robot consciousness. I mean, we have also already seen that most materialists wish to allow for multiple realizability. However, there are surely limits here for any materialist too. After all, a materialist does not have to allow that *any* kind of physical stuff, even properly interconnected, can produce consciousness any more than any type of physical substance can, say, conduct electricity. Could consciousness be duplicated by a clever and sophisticated arrangement of paper clips and beer cans? Probably not.

DAVE: Maybe the real problem is how and when we should distinguish mere "simulation" of thinking or consciousness from genuine "duplication"? Much like we might say that a computerized hurricane or fire simulation does not *duplicate* a real hurricane or fire—you won't get wet or burned!—perhaps the same goes for any alleged computer "mental" activity. We do, for example, distinguish between real diamonds or leather and mere simulations of them which are not the real thing.

STEVE: Yeah, but sometimes a simulation can be a duplication, for example, some artificially produced coal in a lab might be called "simulated" coal but yet it is still "real" coal in the sense that it's physically indistinguishable from what we get out of the ground. And what about, say, artificial light? Isn't artificial light still really light? A genuine duplication might just be created through nonnatural means.

DAVE: Interesting. I suppose that we can't just assume that simulations of thinking will always be *mere* simulations and could *never* be the real thing. The problem with mental states is that we would seemingly first need to know what the essence of 'thinking' or 'consciousness' is before we can know if we have a simulation or duplication. For this reason and because there is so much disagreement about the essential nature of mental states, it is difficult to see how this can be settled anytime soon. After all, we are still trying to understand what exactly makes *our* mental states conscious.

STEVE: Good point.

MARY: Yeah. But aside from lacking an organic brain, why else might we rule out machine or robot consciousness?

DAVE: I have a very different second reason. Machines do not really *understand* anything that is going on inside them. There is merely the manipulation of symbols and programmed functioning, but no real understanding of internal processes. In short, a machine does not understand the meaning of anything it processes.

STEVE: You mean in the way we consciously understand the workings of our own minds through introspection?

DAVE: Sure. I'll first modify an argument given by philosopher John Searle in a paper I just read: Suppose we could make a robot that serves as an excellent translator of German. Whenever it's given a German sentence as input it responds with the perfect German output. It can answer questions flawlessly in German. Would we say that the robot *understands* or *knows* German? Of course not.

STEVE: I agree. This is related to conditions two and three. If we built a robot which nonverbally and verbally behaved as we do in giving correct German translations or responses, we should still not say that it understands German. This clear lack of understanding on the part of the robot itself is good reason to doubt that it is conscious.

DAVE: Right. Searle himself uses his now famous **Chinese Room Argument** thought experiment where he is in a room and follows English instructions for manipulating Chinese symbols in order to produce appropriate answers to questions in Chinese. He argues that, despite the appearance of understanding Chinese—say, from outside the room—he does not understand Chinese at all. He is merely manipulating symbols. This is precisely what computers do and so no computer, merely by following a program, genuinely understands anything.

MARY: Well, I'm not sure that we shouldn't properly attribute some form of "understanding" to your robot, Steve, or to the entire room, Dave.

DAVE: Really? Does a chess machine really understand the rules of chess? Does a calculator understand mathematics?

MARY: Maybe not, but if there were a robot that was behaviorally indistinguishable from humans in all or most respects, then it would be reasonable. I'm not saying there is such a robot now, but surely there could be.

DAVE: I don't see how, especially if you mean anything like a conscious understanding.

STEVE: I agree with Dave, especially given our other earlier reason.

DAVE: Let me elaborate on the larger point in Searle's argument. He is mainly concerned with rejecting what he calls **strong AI**, which is the view that suitably programmed computers literally have a mind; that is, they really understand language and actually have other mental capacities similar to humans. This is contrasted with "weak AI," which is the view that computers are merely useful tools for studying the mind. Programs that are implemented by computers are purely syntactical and so computer operations are merely "formal" in the sense that they respond only to the physical form of the strings of symbols, not to the meaning of the symbols. Syntax is only about symbols, sentences, and grammatical structure. Minds, on the other hand, have mental states with real meaning.

STEVE: Interesting. Go on.

DAVE: We associate meanings with the words or signs in language and we respond to signs because of their meaning, not just their physical appearance. In short, we understand the symbols and computers don't. The key point is that syntax is not by itself sufficient for semantics. So although computers may be able to manipulate symbols to produce appropriate responses to natural language input, such as German, they don't understand the sentences they receive or send out since they can't associate meanings with the words.

STEVE: I see.

DAVE: So no matter how intelligent a computer behaves, since the symbols it processes are meaningless to it, it's not really intelligent. Its internal states and processes, being purely syntactic, lack semantics or meaning and so it doesn't really have meaningful intentional mental states, such as thoughts, beliefs, and desires.

MARY: But, again, aren't there degrees of "understanding"? Why can't there be unconscious understanding? Or do you always mean something like the "conscious grasping of meaning" when you use the term "understanding"?

DAVE: Good questions. It does seem to come back to consciousness in the end, doesn't it? I know that Searle acknowledged that there are degrees of understanding, but he argues that there are still clear cases in which 'understanding' does not apply.

MARY: So, in a way, we are back to our four conditions?

STEVE: How so?

MARY: I mean, how would we even know if we created a conscious robot? Is the ability to communicate and behave like us enough to indicate consciousness? How could we know if a robot really experiences pains or various emotions? We could ask a robot if it's conscious but will that really help?

STEVE: I do want to point out that the growing areas of cognitive science and artificial intelligence can importantly bear on philosophical questions of consciousness. Much of the more recent research focuses on how to program a computer to model more closely the workings of the human brain. There are so-called neural nets or **connectionist networks** with nodes analogous to neurons and connections analogous to neural connections. There are patterns of activity in neural networks that mimic the way our neurons work in at least some ways. There are actually no explicit inner representations or symbols. Perhaps this is the better way to approach the research.

MARY: Right, this frequently goes hand in hand with the development in labs of so-called social robots, such as ASIMO developed by Honda. They are quite humanlike and even, some might say, a bit creepy. One central related idea is that a real mind can only be created by interacting with the environment in real time. Those working in bio-robotics will, for example, build machines which model the way that biological organisms develop and behave. So robots can learn over time, much like our children do, to walk, to catch a ball, or to follow instructions.

DAVE: Interesting, but I still do worry about the potential ethical dangers of creating potentially autonomous moral agents so that a robot could shut down an electrical power grid or even commit terrorist acts when used in place of humans in a decision-making role. But if consciousness is necessary for being held morally responsible, then we must be careful not to put the cart before the horse.

MARY: And let's not forget the related worry of creating a kind of slave class of conscious robots who themselves don't have any rights or protection. Much like animals, if we really come to believe that robots are conscious, then this should have at least some bearing on how we should treat them. Shouldn't we care if robots really can suffer and feel pain? Maybe they could even get depressed or suicidal? Will they have "free will" in some sense of that term? If so, might we be in danger, especially if they are stronger and more intelligent than us?

STEVE: Conversely, perhaps our minds can even eventually be downloaded into a machine for permanent safekeeping so that a kind of digital immortality can be achieved. It seems farfetched but you never know.

DAVE: Whoa. That's a wild thought.

STEVE: It's also possible that we'll morph into machines ourselves through the regular replacement of our body parts over time. But being able to replace neurons and their activity is of course the real difficulty. It's hard to know now just how likely these futuristic scenarios are. Check out the work of Ray Kurzweil who has a lot to say about various future scenarios and is much more optimistic than many others.

MARY: I will.   .

3.5 The Inverted Spectrum Problem

STEVE: Anyway, we did seem to agree earlier that the second subquestion is very difficult, if not impossible, to answer regarding aliens and even some lower animals.

DAVE: Sure.

MARY: Especially for aliens.

STEVE: But I think that this problem can even be serious with respect to other humans. Even if we're confident that other humans have conscious minds, there remains one special kind of skepticism.

MARY: What?

STEVE: Well, one way of putting the problem is this: How do I know, for example, that you have the same color experience that I do when I am perceiving a ripe tomato? I know what my inner color experience is like, but can I know that yours is anything like mine?

DAVE: Surely it's reasonable to assume that we all have the same kind of "reddish" color experience.

STEVE: I don't think so.

MARY: Why not?

STEVE: Let me put it this way: Pretend that we have a ripe tomato and a lemon on this table. When I perceive the tomato I know what my color experience is like and I call it 'red'; and when I look at the lemon I know what that experience is like and I call it 'yellow.' But how could I know that when you perceive these items you're having the same kinds of inner experiences? In fact, how do I know that your color experiences aren't the opposite of mine or "inverted" with respect to mine?

MARY: You mean that I might perceive the lemon color the way that you perceive the tomato color?

STEVE: Yes, and vice versa. And perhaps there are many humans who perceive colors in this inverted way. How could we know otherwise?

DAVE: Interesting. I see what you mean. I assume this problem could arise in terms of the other senses.

STEVE: Sure. I could have talked about "taste inversion" by using different flavors, or discussed "hearing inversion" by using different sounds. But let's stick to visual color inversion. This is called the **inverted spectrum problem**.

MARY: But don't we know the answer on the basis of verbal behavior?

STEVE: Such as?

MARY: We all say that the tomato looks red like blood; not yellow like the sun. If you ask me what color the tomato is, I will say 'red,' just as you will.

STEVE: But that's only what we say. I'm talking about the inner color *experience*, not the *name* we use for it. All I would know is that you use the word 'red' to describe what you perceive the color of a tomato to be, but I know nothing about what your color experience itself is like.

DAVE: That's true. After all, how are we taught color terms?

STEVE: Exactly. We put different objects in front of children and teach them to associate color terms with them. For example, a child is told that a tomato and a fire truck are red, and a lemon and the sun are yellow. And so on. But this tells us nothing about how these objects appear to the children in their own subjective experience. So we all grow up using the words in a consistent way, but we have no basis for knowing that our color experiences are the same. It's a bit like the "absent qualia" worry we had last night about functionalism except that this is a qualia inversion. That is, there could be functionally and behaviorally equivalent humans who experience colors differently in a systematic way.

DAVE: So what Mary might call 'red' when she looks at the tomato could still appear to her the way that lemons appear to us.

STEVE: Sure. You see how difficult it is to know otherwise?

MARY: But wouldn't there be other evidence that could help decide the issue?

STEVE: Like what? After all, it's difficult to explain to another person what a color looks like. Try it sometime.

MARY: True, but we might associate other words and even some emotions with the experience of a certain color.

DAVE: For example?

MARY: We might say that some colors are light, dark, strong, weak, dull, bright, and so on. So if we hear two people comparing color experiences, we should be able to make substantial headway.

DAVE: You mean like ruling out a 'brown-red' inversion by asking them which object looks 'bright' or 'dark'?

MARY: Yeah, something like that. If they agree on which object looks bright, then we certainly have good evidence for their having similar color experiences. Right?

STEVE: Maybe, but it wouldn't work for a 'yellow-red' case. And the point made earlier goes for how we learn these words. We are taught to associate the term 'bright' with red and yellow experiences and 'dark' with brown color experiences. But, once again, we have no clue as to what another's experience itself is like.

MARY: But don't you think this problem could be overcome? I mean, are there whole groups of painters and artists out there experiencing the world in such radically different ways? I find that hard to believe. Wouldn't there have to be some outward sign of it?

STEVE: I'm not so sure. But, anyway, we obviously don't normally quiz each other in order to find out such things. So our knowledge of another human's color experience is rather shaky. I can't think of any other way to help us deal with the problem.

MARY: Perhaps neurophysiological evidence can help settle the issue.

DAVE: How?

MARY: We have good evidence that certain neurons and "cones" are typically involved in the visual processing of certain types of color experience.

DAVE: So?

MARY: Well, if another human being's brain works the way ours does while looking at the ripe tomato, it seems reasonable to conclude that he's having a similar kind of "reddish" experience. I mean, if neurons fire in those same areas all across the human species, doesn't that point to a similarity in the experiences themselves?

DAVE: I don't see why. First of all, when we look at another's brain, we don't actually see the color as he perceives it. All we see is the brain, which is the same color through and through; it's not as if those neurons become red when they fire.

MARY: Of course, but there is the association between the neural firings and that type of color experience.

DAVE: But we must eventually rely on the subject's verbal reports in order to make the correlations. And so we end up right back with the same old problem.

MARY: Really? I would think that such a uniform objective fact about human brains would outweigh any doubt arising from our earlier problem.

STEVE: Maybe it would, but I don't know how strongly to weigh such evidence. Also, we might then ask: How do we know that all human brains are "wired" in the same way? Maybe a certain small percentage of humans have brains in which the neurons that typically underlie red experiences instead underlie yellow experiences. That is, maybe some human brains themselves are wired in an inverted way. We certainly can't know otherwise by simply looking at them. As Dave said, we won't see the color of the person's experience simply by observing the relevant neural firings.

MARY: This sounds a little crazy to me, but I do see your concern. Anyway, I'm a bit tired. I think I'll go home. Maybe I'll stare at my nice *brown* carpet for a while and think about this some more.

DAVE: OK. I'll give you both a ride home if you want. I haven't been drinking.

STEVE: Good, thanks. Let's talk again some other time. I'm really looking forward to taking more courses in philosophy of mind and consciousness.

MARY: Me too. It's been great so far and I really love how it overlaps with psychology and neuropsychology. Unfortunately, I do have that funeral tomorrow for my cousin. I guess death is a part of life, isn't it? Very sad though.

DAVE: Yes, especially when we feel that a life is cut short so early and tragically.

STEVE: I think we can all agree on that.

BIBLIOGRAPHY AND SUGGESTIONS FOR FURTHER READING

Introductory Books

Bermúdez, J. L. 2014. *Cognitive Science: An Introduction to the Science of the Mind*, 2nd ed. Cambridge: Cambridge University Press.

Blackmore, S. 2019. *Consciousness: An Introduction*, 3rd ed. New York: Routledge Press.

Churchland, P. M. 2013. *Matter and Consciousness*, 3rd ed. Cambridge, MA: MIT Press.

Gennaro, R. 2017. *Consciousness*. New York: Routledge Press.

Heil, J. 2019. *Philosophy of Mind*, 4th ed. New York: Routledge Press

Kim, J. 2010. *Philosophy of Mind*, 3rd ed. New York: Routledge Press.

Perry, J. 2018. *Dialogue on Consciousness: Minds, Brains, and Zombies*. Indianapolis: Hackett Publishing Company.

Ramachandran, V. S. 2004. *A Brief Tour of Human Consciousness*. New York: PI Press.

Revonsuo, A. 2010. *Consciousness: The Science of Subjectivity*. New York: Psychology Press.

Seager, W. 2016. *Theories of Consciousness*, 2nd ed. New York and London: Routledge.

Searle, J. 2004. *Mind: A Brief Introduction*. New York: Oxford University Press.

Weisberg, J. 2014. *Consciousness*. Malden, MA: Polity Press.

Anthologies

Alter, T., and Howell, R. eds. 2012. *Consciousness and the Mind-Body Problem.* New York: Oxford University Press.

Alter, T., and Walter, S. eds. 2007. *Phenomenal Concepts and Phenomenal Knowledge: New Essays on Consciousness and Physicalism.* Oxford: Oxford University Press.

Baars, B., Banks, W., and Newman, J. eds. 2003. *Essential Sources in the Scientific Study of Consciousness.* Cambridge, MA: MIT Press.

Block, N., Flanagan, O., and Güzeledere, G., eds. 1997. *The Nature of Consciousness.* Cambridge, MA: MIT Press.

Chalmers, D., ed. 2002. *Philosophy of Mind: Classical and Contemporary Readings.* New York: Oxford University Press.

Cleeremans, A., ed. 2003. *The Unity of Consciousness: Binding, Integration and Dissociation.* Oxford: Oxford University Press.

Gennaro, R., ed. 2015. *Disturbed Consciousness: New Essays on Psychopathology and Theories of Consciousness.* Cambridge, MA: MIT Press.

Gennaro, R., ed. 2018. *The Routledge Handbook of Consciousness.* New York: Routledge Press, 2018.

Laureys, S., ed. 2005. *The Boundaries of Consciousness: Neurobiology and Neuropathology.* Oxford: Elsevier.

Martin, M. and Augustine, K. eds. 2015. *The Myth of an Afterlife.* New York: Rowman and Littlefield.

Metzinger, T., ed. 2000. *Neural Correlates of Consciousness: Empirical and Conceptual Questions.* Cambridge, MA: MIT Press.

Shear, J., ed. 1997. *Explaining Consciousness: The Hard Problem.* Cambridge, MA: MIT Press.

Velmans, M., and Schneider, S. eds. 2007. *The Blackwell Companion to Consciousness.* Malden, MA: Blackwell.

Zelazo, P., Moscovitch, M., and Thompson, E., eds. 2007. *The Cambridge Handbook of Consciousness.* Cambridge, MA: Cambridge University Press.

There are also many useful articles with expansive references in the online *Stanford Encyclopedia of Philosophy* (http://plato.stanford.edu/) and the *Internet Encyclopedia of Philosophy* (http://www.iep.utm.edu/). Moreover, specialized journals such as *Philosophical Psychology, Mind and Language, Journal of Consciousness Studies, Consciousness and Cognition,* and the *Neuroscience of Consciousness* have offered quality places for disseminating work in the field. The same is true for the wonderful database and bibliography *PhilPapers* (http://philpapers.org/).

Advanced Books

Baars, B., and Gage, N. 2010. *Cognition, Brain, and Consciousness: Introduction to Cognitive Neuroscience*, 2nd ed. Oxford: Elselvier.

Block, N. 2007. *Consciousness, Function, and Representation: Collected Papers* (Volume 1). Cambridge, MA: MIT Press/Bradford Books

Chalmers, D. 1996. *The Conscious Mind*. Oxford: Oxford University Press.

Dennett, D. 1991. *Consciousness Explained*. New York: Little, Brown and Co.

Flanagan, O. 1992. *Consciousness Reconsidered*. Cambridge, MA: MIT Press/ Bradford Books.

Gennaro, R. 2012. *The Consciousness Paradox: Consciousness, Concepts, and Higher-Order Thoughts*. Cambridge, MA: MIT Press.

Graham, G. 2013. *The Disordered Mind: An Introduction into Philosophy of Mind and Mental Illness*, 2nd ed. London: Routledge.

Levine, J. 2001. *Purple Haze: The Puzzle of Conscious Experience*. Cambridge, MA: MIT Press.

McGinn, C. 1991. *The Problem of Consciousness*. Cambridge, MA: Blackwell.

Nichols, S. and Stich, S. 2003. *Mindreading*. New York: Oxford University Press.

Pereboom, D. 2011. *Consciousness and the Prospects for Physicalism*. New York: Oxford University Press.

Polger, T. 2004. *Natural Minds*. Cambridge, MA: MIT Press.

Prinz, J. 2012. *The Conscious Brain*. New York: Oxford University Press.

Searle, J. 1992. *The Rediscovery of the Mind*. Cambridge, MA: MIT Press/ Bradford Books.

Van Inwagen, P. 1998. *The Possibility of Resurrection and Other Essays in Christian Apologetics*. Boulder, CO: Westview Press.

For more on Descartes' early dualist arguments, see his *Meditations on First Philosophy*, translated by Donald A. Cress (Indianapolis: Hackett Publishing Company, 1979). For a more recent defense of interactionism, see Karl R. Popper and John C. Eccles, *The Self and its Brain* (London: Routledge and Kegan Paul, 1977).

Dave's story about Maria in the Second Night was intentionally modeled after Frank Jackson's thought experiment about Mary in: Jackson, F.

1982. Epiphenomenal Qualia. *Philosophical Quarterly* 32: 127–136. It is sometimes called the "knowledge argument" against materialism. See also:

Horgan, T. 1984. Jackson on Physical Information and Qualia. *Philosophical Quarterly* 34: 147–152.

Jackson, F. 1986. What Mary Didn't Know. *Journal of Philosophy* 83: 291–295.

Ludlow, P., Nagasawa, Y., and Stoljar, D. eds. 2004. *There's Something about Mary*. Cambridge, MA: MIT Press.

Perry, J. 2001. *Knowledge, Possibility, and Consciousness*. Cambridge, MA: MIT Press.

Steve's story about the cat in the Second Night was modeled after Thomas Nagel's argument in: Nagel, T. 1974. What Is it Like to Be a Bat? *Philosophical Review* 83: 435–450. See also:

Levine, J. 1983. Materialism and Qualia: The Explanatory Gap. *Pacific Philosophical Quarterly* 64: 354–361.

For more on animal mentality and consciousness, see:

Andrews, K. 2015. *The Animal Mind: An Introduction to the Philosophy of Animal Cognition*. New York: Routledge.

Beck, J., and Andrews, K. eds. 2017. *Routledge Handbook of Philosophy of Animal Minds*. New York: Routledge Publishers.

Gennaro, R. 2018. "Animal Consciousness," in the *Encyclopedia of Animal Cognition and Behavior*, edited by J. Vonk and T. Shackelford. New York: Springer.

Hurley, S., and Nudds, M. eds. 2006. *Rational Animals?* New York: Oxford University Press.

Lurz, R., ed. 2009. *The Philosophy of Animal Minds*. Cambridge, MA: Cambridge University Press.

Terrace, H., and Metcalfe, J. eds. 2005. *The Missing Link in Cognition: Origins of Self-Reflective Consciousness*. New York: Oxford University Press.

Tye, M. 2016. *Tense Bees and Shell-Shocked Crabs*. Oxford: Oxford University Press.

See also the online journal *Animal Sentience* at: https://animalstudiesrepository.org/animsent/

Dave's story about the robot German translator in the Third Night is based on John Searle's very well-known Chinese Room Argument in: Searle, J. 1980. Minds, Brains and Programs. *Behavioral and Brain Sciences* 3: 417–457.

For more on the problem of machine consciousness and artificial intelligence, see:

Boden, M., ed. 1990. *The Philosophy of Artificial Intelligence.* New York: Oxford University Press.

Haugeland, J. 1985. *Artificial Intelligence: The Very Idea.* Cambridge, MA: MIT Press.

Kurzweil, R. 2005. *The Singularity Is Near: When Humans Transcend Biology.* New York: Penguin.

Preston, J., and Bishop, J. eds. 2002. *Views into the Chinese Room: New Essays on Searle and Artificial Intelligence.* New York: Oxford University Press.

Saygin, A., Cicekli, I., and Akman, V. 2000. Turing Test: 50 Years Later. *Minds and Machines* 10: 463–518.

Searle, J. 1984. *Minds, Brains, and Science.* Cambridge, MA: Harvard University Press.

Turing, A. 1950. Computing Machinery and Intelligence. *Mind* 59: 433–460.

Wallach, W., and Allen, C. 2010. *Moral Machines: Teaching Robots Right from Wrong.* New York: Oxford University Press.

Waskan, J. 2010. Connectionism. *Internet Encyclopedia of Philosophy.* Available at: http://www.iep.utm.edu/connect/

STUDY QUESTIONS

THE FIRST NIGHT

1. What is materialism? What is substance dualism? Why does Mary believe that it is almost impossible for a materialist to believe in immortality? Why is a dualist in a better position to believe in immortality?

2. Do you agree with Mary that it is difficult to make any coherent distinction between the mind and the soul? Why or why not?

3. Explain in some detail the three general scientific reasons Mary gives in favor of materialism. Do you find these reasons compelling? Which do you think is the strongest? Does Dave satisfactorily respond? Why or why not?

4. State and explain the Divisibility Argument for dualism. Explain the role of Leibniz's Law in the argument. Discuss in some detail several objections to it. Does Dave satisfactorily respond? Why or why not?

5. State and explain the Argument from Introspection. Explain the role of Leibniz's Law in the argument. Discuss in some detail the two major objections to it, paying special attention to the failure of Leibniz's Law in intensional contexts. Can Dave satisfactorily respond? Why or why not?

THE SECOND NIGHT

1. What is interactionism? Explain, in general, why Mary believes that materialism can explain mind-body interaction far better than substance dualism can.

2. Explain in some detail the specific objections to interactionism, including the argument from brain damage. Does Dave satisfactorily respond to either objection? Why or why not?

3. What is parallelism? Why doesn't Dave consider it the right version of substance dualism? Explain several objections to parallelism. Do you think that epiphenomenalism or property dualism fare better?

4. What is type-type materialism? Why doesn't Mary believe that this is the correct version of materialism? What is token-token materialism? How does it avoid the major problem with type-materialism? Is it really a preferable position? Is functionalism any better?

5. What is the materialist problem of consciousness and the so-called knowledge argument against materialism? Explain in some detail the two stories used by Dave and Steve to illustrate this problem. What three responses does Mary offer? Does she successfully respond? Why or why not? Can you think of any other possible responses?

THE THIRD NIGHT

1. What is the problem of other minds? What are the two subproblems and why is it important to distinguish between them? What is inductive knowledge? Why is it relevant to the problem of other minds?

2. Why does Mary think that the problem of other minds is more difficult to solve for a dualist? Is she right? Why or why not?

3. Describe the four conditions or types of evidence that can help us solve the problem of other minds. Which do you think is strongest? Why? Which do you think is weakest? Why? Use examples.

4. How does Steve critique each of the four conditions individually? How do Mary and Dave reply to Steve's critique? What is the relevance of Mary's analogy of the prosecutor building a case against a defendant?

5. Can we know that other humans have conscious minds? On what grounds?

6. Can we know that animals have conscious minds? If so, which animals and on what grounds? Which animals or creatures are you most skeptical about? Why?

7. Explain Steve's story about the aliens. Would we be able to determine whether or not they are conscious creatures? Why or why not?

8. Why do Steve and Dave doubt that a machine or robot can be conscious? Does Mary satisfactorily respond? Why or why not? Who do you think is closer to the truth? Do you think that biology is essential to consciousness? Why or why not?

9. Explain the inverted spectrum problem. Why is it most relevant to the second subproblem? Does Mary satisfactorily respond? Why or why not? Can you think of any other responses?

GLOSSARY

absent qualia argument: An objection to functionalism which asserts that it is possible to have two functionally equivalent creatures where one of them lacks qualia entirely. There could be creatures, functionally equivalent to normal humans, whose mental states have no qualitative character at all.

agnosia: A loss of ability to *recognize* objects, persons, sounds, shapes, or smells while the specific sense itself is not defective.

binding problem: The problem of how the brain integrates information processed by different regions of the brain into a unified experience.

Chinese Room Argument: John Searle's argument based on imagining himself running a program for using Chinese and then showing that he does not understand Chinese. Strong AI is false because merely running the program does not result in any real understanding. Searle utilizes a thought experiment whereby he is in a room and follows English instructions for manipulating Chinese symbols in order to produce appropriate answers to questions in Chinese.

connectionist networks: The approach to AI where the emphasis is on patterns of neural activity augmented by backpropagation and resulting in concept learning and application. This approach is also sometimes called Parallel Distributed Processing (PDP) and attempts to explain human abilities by using artificial neural networks (or "neural nets"). Neural networks are simplified models of the brain composed of large numbers of neuronlike units (or "nodes"), together with weights that measure the strength of connections between the units. There are patterns of activity in neural networks that mimic the way our neurons work in at least some ways. There are actually no explicit inner representations or symbols.

conscious ("what it is like" sense): Thomas Nagel's famous description that when I am in a conscious mental state, there is "something it is like" for me to be in that state from the subjective or first-person point of view.

consciousness, hard problem of: Coined by David Chalmers, this refers to the difficulty of explaining just how physical processes in the brain give rise to subjective conscious experiences.

consciousness, materialist problem of: The alleged inability of materialism to reduce consciousness to something in physical terms or to explain consciousness in neurophysiological terms.

consciousness, unity of: There are many different senses of "unity" of consciousness but perhaps most common is the notion that, from the first-person point of view, we experience the world in an integrated way and as a single phenomenal field of experience.

Conservation of Energy, Principle of: The total amount of energy in the universe, or any controlled part of it, remains constant.

dissociative identity disorder (DID): A psychiatric diagnosis describing a condition in which a person displays multiple distinct identities (known as 'alters' or 'parts'), each with its own pattern of perceiving and interacting with the environment. DID was previously called "multiple personality disorder."

dualism (general): The view that the conscious mind or a conscious mental state is non-physical in some sense.

dualism, interactionist (or simply "interactionism"): The most common form of "substance dualism" and its name derives from the widely accepted fact that mental states and bodily states causally interact with each other. It is sometimes referred to as "Cartesian dualism" due to the influence of Descartes.

dualism, property: The view that there are mental *properties* (i.e., characteristics or aspects of things), as opposed to substances, that are neither identical with nor reducible to physical properties.

dualism, substance: The view that the mind is a nonphysical substance distinct from the body.

epiphenomenalism: The view that mental events are caused by, but not reducible to, brain events such that mental events are mere "epiphenomena." Mental states or events are caused by physical states or events in the brain but do not themselves cause anything.

explanatory gap: Joseph Levine's way of expressing the difficulty for any materialistic attempt to explain consciousness due to the gap in our ability to explain the connection between phenomenal properties and brain properties.

frame problem: One of the obstacles to programming a system to focus only on *relevant* information when attempting to solve a problem.

functionalism: The view that conscious mental states should only be identified with the functional role they play within an organism rather than what physically makes them up.

intensional contexts: Instances where replacing one co-referring term with another can change a statement's truth-value. One such context involves sentences with mental expressions such as 'believes that,' 'conceives that,' 'thinks that,' 'knows that,' etc.

inverted spectrum problem: An objection to functionalism which maintains that there could be an individual who, for example, satisfies the functional definition of our experience of red but is experiencing yellow, and yet is behaviorally indistinguishable from someone with normal color vision.

knowledge argument: Frank Jackson's argument against materialism which supposes that knowing all the physical facts about conscious experience leaves out "mental facts" or an explanation of the subjective conscious experience.

Leibniz's Law: If x and y have any different properties, then x cannot be identical with y. Alternatively, if an object or event x is identical with an object or event y, then x and y have all of the same properties.

materialism: The view that the mind is the brain or, more specifically, that conscious mental activity is identical with neural activity (sometimes called "identity theory" although there are also other versions of materialism).

materialism, token-token: The view that each particular conscious mental *event* in some organism is identical with some particular brain process or event in that organism.

materialism, type-type: The view that mental *properties*, such as 'having a desire to drink some water' or 'being in pain,' are literally identical with a brain property of some kind.

metaphysics: The branch of philosophy concerned with the ultimate nature of reality.

mindreading: The ability to attribute mental states to others or have a thought about another's mental state.

multiple realizability (of mental states): The view that the same mental state-type can be had by radically different creatures with very different physiologies.

mysterianism: Colin McGinn's view that we are simply not capable of solving the problem of consciousness. Mysterians believe that the hard problem can *never* be solved because of human cognitive limitations.

near-death experience (NDE): This occurs when some patients, often in cardiac arrest at a hospital, experience a peaceful moving through a tunnel-like structure to a light, among other things.

other minds, problem of: Primarily the problem of how we can know that another creature or thing has a conscious mind.

out-of-body experience (OBE): Instances where one seems to perceive the world (and often one's own body) from above or outside one's body.

panpsychism: The view that all things in physical reality, even down to microparticles, have some degree of mentality or consciousness.

parallelism: A version of substance dualism which denies the causal interaction between the nonphysical mental and physical bodily realms (often attributed to Gottfried Leibniz). The idea is that our minds and our bodies run along parallel tracks, so to speak, with each unfolding according to its own laws. Leibniz used the analogy of two watches which are perfectly synchronized so that mental states and bodily states are timed perfectly.

phenomenal concepts: Concepts which use a phenomenal or "first-person" property to refer to some conscious mental state.

prosopagnosia: The inability to recognize familiar faces typically caused by damage to the fusiform gyrus in the occipito-temporal cortex.

qualia (singular, quale): Qualitative or phenomenal properties of mental states. Most often understood as the felt properties or qualities of conscious states.

reductionism: A relation between theories such that one theory (the reduced theory) is derivable from another theory (the reducing theory) usually with the help of "bridging principles."

simplicity, principle of (or "Occam's razor"): If there are two theories, both of which explain the same number of observations or facts, then we should accept the one that posits fewer objects or the one that is more simple.

somatoparaphrenia: A type of delusion where one denies ownership of a limb or an entire side of one's body.

strong AI: The view that suitably programmed computers literally have a mind; that is, they really understand language and actually have other mental capacities similar to humans. This is contrasted with "weak AI," which is the view that computers are merely useful tools for studying the mind.

Turing test: The basic idea is that if a machine could fool an interrogator (who could not see the machine) into thinking that it was human then we should say it thinks or, at least, has intelligence.

INDEX OF KEY TERMS